BALI

AN OPEN FORTRESS, 1995–2005

Administrative areas of Bali

KARANGASEM
Amlapura
Besakih
Klungkung
BANGLI
Padanggalak
beach
Sanur
GIANYAR
Kesiman
BULELENG
Denpasar
Singaraja
BADUNG
Kuta
TABANAN

JEMBRANA
Negara

JAVA
BALI
LOMBOK
SUMBAWA
SUMBA

(Collection of KITLV, Leiden)

BALI

AN OPEN FORTRESS, 1995–2005

Regional Autonomy, Electoral Democracy and
Entrenched Identities

Henk Schulte Nordholt

NUS PRESS
SINGAPORE

© 2007 NUS Press
National University of Singapore
AS3-01-02, 3 Arts Link
Singapore 117569

Fax   : (65) 6774-0652
E-mail : nusbooks@nus.edu.sg
Website : http://www.nus.edu.sg/npu

ISBN 978-9971-69-375-6 (Paper)

National Library Board Singapore Cataloguing in Publication Data

Schulte Nordholt, Henk, 1953–
   Bali, an open fortress, 1995–2005 : regional autonomy, electoral
democracy and entrenched identities / Henk Schulte Nordholt. –
Singapore: NUS Press, c2007.
   p. cm.
   Includes bibliographical references and index.
   ISBN-13 : 978-9971-69-375-6 (pbk.)

   1. Decentralisation in government – Indonesia. 2. Democracy –
Indonesia – Bali (Province). 3. Balinese (Indonesian people) – Ethnic
identity. 4. Bali (Indonesia : Province) – Politics and government.
I. Title.

DS647.B2
320.95986 – dc22   SLS2007029831

Typeset by: International Typesetters Pte Ltd
Printed by: Vetak Services

Contents

List of Illustrations

Acknowledgements

In 2002 the Royal Institute of Southeast Asian and Caribbean Studies (KITLV) in Leiden initiated a new research project, which aimed to analyse the impact of decentralisation and regional autonomy in Indonesia. In the early 1980s I had done historical research on Bali and this project offered me the opportunity to return to this special island.

For a long time Bali was portrayed as a cultural safe haven, but the terrorist attacks in October 2002 and 2005 have challenged that perception. The assaults emphasised the extent to which the population of Bali has faced fundamental challenges as a result of economic, political, and religious changes over the past decade. As an historian with an interest in recent developments I have tried to trace these complex processes, which unfolded at different but interrelated levels.

The information for this book was gathered during visits to Bali in 2003, 2004, 2005, and 2006. Because it was not possible to conduct fieldwork over a longer period of time I had to rely primarily on written sources, but I have tried to talk to many people as well. I could not have accomplished this complex project without the skilful assistance of Drs Nyoman Wijaya, Drs Slamat Trisila, I Made Arsana Dwiputra, Ngurah Suryawan and I Wayan Supartha who helped to collect valuable sets of information on various topics.

ACKNOWLEDGEMENTS

I would also like to thank Margreet Bersma, I Nyoman Darma Putra, Degung Santikarma, Gerry van Klinken, Graeme MacRae, Michel Picard, Carol Warren, Adrian Vickers, and the participants of the workshop "Renegotiating boundaries; Local politics in post-Suharto Indonesia" (20–22 December 2004) at the KITLV office in Jakarta for their helpful comments on earlier drafts. Needless to say that I am responsible for mistakes and opinions expressed in the chapters.

Leiden/Singapore, September 2006

CHAPTER 1

In Search of Stability

On 16 August 2003 the *Bali Post* celebrated its 55th anniversary with a special edition. It contained an extensive report on a seminar held earlier that month under the title *Menuju Strategi Ajeg Bali*, "towards a strategy for a strong and resilient Bali".[1] The word *ajeg* refers to a discourse about the position of Balinese culture in present day Indonesia, in particular since *reformasi* and *desentralisasi* changed the political map of Indonesia. *Reformasi* opened hopes for a more democratic system in Indonesia after Suharto stepped down as president in May 1998, and in 1999 laws on administrative decentralisation, or *desentralisasi*, promised devolution of power, resulting in regional autonomy bringing government closer to people.[2] Nevertheless the general feeling at the seminar was that Bali was endangered by a variety of negative external influences and that Balinese culture had to be rescued.

Representatives from the tourist sector, economists, and experts in fields such as agriculture, education, the performing arts and architecture voiced a shared concern that uncontrolled building activities and the rapidly expanding tourist sector were causing large-scale environmental damage. They also feared that Western influences stimulate criminality, the use of narcotics, and a hedonistic materialistic attitude, at the cost of traditional religious Balinese values. At the same time, the influx of thousands of Muslim migrant workers from the neighbouring islands of Java and Lombok are causing the unpleasant feeling that Balinese are becoming a minority on their own island. In order to counter the inflow of these "foreigners", as well as the impact of foreign capital and the concomitant commoditisation of their culture, among Balinese intellectuals the need was felt for a spiritual revitalisation and the strengthening of cultural self-confidence, while they emphasised the importance of local knowledge and the central role of customary institutions. Terms used in this context include "quality tourism", "a Balinese culture landscape", "a Balinese economy informed by religious principles". *Ajeg* Bali became the key word in a quest for a new master plan that respected the delicate balance between Gods, men and environment (*Tri Hita Karana*). Such were the concerns of predominantly urban middle-class Balinese meeting each other on a regular basis at seminars hosted in five star hotels.

The discourse on *Ajeg* Bali has a long history, and is closely connected with efforts by outside forces to define the unique (non-Islamic, Hindu) identity of the Balinese. Especially from the 1930s onwards, the Dutch colonial administration took steps to preserve Bali in a "steady state" of supposed well-balanced authenticity while at the same time introducing a set of new categories which invited Balinese to think about themselves. In order to preserve the special customary arrangements an institutional distinction was made at the village level between custom (*adat*) and administration (*dinas*). Custom, or tradition, was framed by religion (*agama*), while later on the notions of culture (*kebudayaan*) and art (*kesenian*) were added as separate categories. Consequently, Balinese started to think about themselves in terms defined by outsiders and, according to Michel Picard, discovered that they had a culture — to be more precise: art, which was turned into a separate entity that could be displayed, performed, reproduced and sold.[3]

Since the 1970s tourism has become a part of Balinese culture. The notion of cultural tourism, which was developed at that time, implied not only the commoditisation of culture but also the touristification of society, blurring artificial boundaries between culture (inside) and tourism (outside). Tourism thus contributed to the making of a Balinese culture that became a marketable object.[4]

In 1958 Bali became a separate province. It was said that leaders of the Islamic party Masyumi had supported this separation

2

because it enabled them to dominate the newly-formed province of Nusa Tenggara Barat, comprising Lombok and Sumbawa.[5] Consequently, Bali showed a rather unique overlap of ethnic and religious identities within a single territorial and administrative unit. However, this seemingly homogeneous unit formed no guarantee for peace and stability, as was rudely illustrated by the mass killings of the mid-1960s.[6]

From the late 1980s onwards, the island came increasingly under pressure as Jakarta-based investors and rising numbers of tourists and migrant workers invaded the island. Were Balinese still in control of their own culture, which formed the backbone of their economy? Two other factors increased the sense of crisis and insecurity among Balinese. The decentralisation laws (no. 22 and 25/1999) promised more autonomy but also brought administrative fragmentation and confusion, and the bomb attack in Legian on 12 October 2002 ruined the image of Bali as a peaceful resort isolated from international terrorism. A second attack on the first of October 2005 — just before the Islamic fasting month and the Balinese day of *Galungan*, when gods and ancestors descend to their temples — reminded the Balinese once more of the precarious volatility of their security.

In this context "*Ajeg*" has become a catchword to indicate the need for a socio-cultural self-defence. However, apart from good but vaguely phrased intentions to strengthen Balinese culture, very few practical solutions were suggested by the participants in the August 2003 *Bali Post* seminar. In the end two dilemmas surfaced. The first was how to achieve greater regional autonomy *vis-à-vis* Jakarta, given that decentralisation had produced administrative fragmentation, which made coordinated action at the provincial level an illusion; second, how to get rid of dangerous external influences and unwanted immigrants, without harming the Balinese economy which needs foreign visitors, investors and cheap labour to survive. The dilemma, in short, was how to make Bali into an open fortress.

For many Balinese, recent developments have been a confusing experience. It looks as if various seemingly unrelated and diffuse processes are at work with highly uncertain outcomes. In the following pages, I intend to trace some of these processes and investigate to what extent they are interrelated. Before I concentrate in Chapter 6 on the phenomenon of *Ajeg* Bali, I will first explore the broader economic and political context in which it eventually emerged as a meaningful concept. In Chapter 2, I trace recent shifts in economic and political relationships between Bali and Jakarta and I will look at the way Balinese tried to cope with the terrorist attack of October 2002. I will in particular look at the impact of political reform and administrative decentralisation in Bali. In Chapter 3, I will focus to the effects of these changes on the politics of caste, the position of regional aristocracies, and the formation of new party-based political alignments. In Bali, decentralisation did not stop at the district level but affected arrangements in the villages as well. What were the implications of these changes in terms of local autonomy and conflict management? In this context it is important to look at long-term trends, which were only accelerated by the recent agony of decentralisation and reform.

In Chapters 4 and 5, I will show that political changes introduced new forms of violence which produced a hightened sense of insecurity. And this provided the very basis for the *Ajeg* Bali movement. I argue that it would be misleading to focus exclusively on the special nature of Bali, as "Baliologists" tend to do. Instead I want to highlight some "Indonesian" phenomena in present day Bali: ethnic tensions, the "sweeping" of immigrants, connections between gangs of *preman* (thugs) and politicians and recent electoral politics. More specifically it is relevant to point at the wider Indonesian context of identity politics and the question which groups are actually involved in the process of authorising culture.[7]

In most publications on the impact of decentralisation and regional autonomy in Indonesia, emphasis is placed on shifts in political and economic relationships and the role of aristocratic and/ or bureaucratic elites. In Chapter 6, I focus my attention on the role of urban middle-class intellectuals in Bali. Whereas in the old days the Balinese kings authorised culture, and Brahmans became more influential during the colonial period and under the New Order, in contemporary Bali, concerned urban middle-class intellectuals position themselves at the forefront of new identity politics. I will concentrate on the role of these intellectuals and their efforts to articulate new exclusive identities.

In Chapter 7, I analyse the role *Ajeg* Bali played in national and regional elections in the period 2003–5, when violence decreased, electoral democracy gained ground and new political leaders emerged. Finally in Chapter 8, I put recent developments in Bali in a broader Indonesian context. The discourse of the urban intellectuals in Bali is deeply rooted in New Order concepts with which they were brought up. As such, their thinking is heavily influenced by an interesting mixture of colonial categories, New Order bureaucratic concepts and recent modernist Hindu ideas. It is against the backdrop of these developments that not only the discussions about *Ajeg* Bali, but also its post-New Order nature should be understood. This raises the question of how *Indonesian* the *Ajeg* Bali movement actually is.

CHAPTER 2

Turbulence and Change

S ince the mid-1990s, Bali has experienced a series of profound changes that were to a large extent determined by the evolving relationship between Jakarta and Bali. I will briefly review developments in the tourist sector, which resulted in protest movements against Jakarta-based investors, the effects of the "Bali Bomb" of October 2002, and finally the impact of the fall of Suharto and the demise of his ruling Golkar party on power relationships in Bali.

Figures of Change[1]

One of the key questions regarding the development of tourism in Bali was: how to profit from tourists while at the same time keeping them at a safe distance? Around 1970, a master plan was designed that concentrated mass tourism in the southern tip of Bali, in the Nusa Dua region of the district of Badung. Due to pressure from other districts, which felt left out, and because domestic tourism and low budget facilities had already developed outside the designated area, Governor Ida Bagus Mantra subsequently opened nine additional tourist localities, and his successor Ida Bagus Oka added 15 more locations in 1988. Development of the tourist sector was accelerated by the deregulation of the banking sector, which facilitated a sharp increase of private domestic investments. When Governor Oka allowed the opening of another six tourist areas in 1993, bringing the total to one quarter of the island, the touristification of Bali accelerated rapidly.[2]

In a relatively short period of time the Balinese economy became heavily dependent on the tourist industry, which was primarily fuelled by an increase of direct foreign arrivals. Two million foreign tourists visited Bali in 2000, compared to one million in 1991 and 300,000 in 1980. Moreover, the number of domestic tourists, who are not included in the official statistics, increased significantly in the early 1990s and even exceeded the number of foreign visitors. It is estimated that in 2001 the total number of tourists was close to three million, which even surpasses the total population of Bali.[3]

	Balinese Population (millions)	Foreign Tourist Arrivals (millions)
1971	2.10	
1980	2.47	0.3
1991	2.70	1.0
2000	3.10	2.0
2001		3.0*
2002	3.20	

Note: *Figure for 2001 is total number of tourists.

The tourist boom had an immediate impact on the environment, the economy and social relationships. The rise in the number of hotel rooms, from 500 in 1970 to 40,000 in 2002, was accompanied by a rapid increase in restaurants, art shops and so-called *ruko* (*rumah toko*, a combination of a shop and a house, on top of which the house temple is built). As a result of these building activities, every year approximately 1,000 hectares of irrigated rice-land has disappeared. In 2001 only 86,000 ha of rice land remained. The traditional landscape has become such a rare commodity that it is now part of one-day bus tours ("Mountain temple, monkey forest, traditional village, *sawah* [rice field] view"). Moreover, ongoing erosion and the large quantities of water needed for hotels and golf courses are likely to cause serious water shortages in the city of Denpasar.

Bali is no longer a predominantly agrarian society. In 2005 half of the population lived in urbanising areas.[4] Between 1970 and 2002 the proportion of the population in the agrarian sector decreased from 56.6 per cent to 21.4 per cent, while those in the tertiary sector — primarily government and tourism — increased from 40.6 per cent to 63.2 per cent. In 1998 51.6 per cent of the Balinese income was derived from tourism, while 40 per cent of the workforce was directly employed in this sector. If related fields like handicraft, garment production and transport are included, 60 to 70 per cent of the workforce depends on tourism.

Export 2003	Value (000 US$)
Garment industry	155,100
Handicraft wood	84,300
Tuna fish	72,700
Furniture	44,000
Handicraft silver	27,000

With an average annual economic growth of about 8 per cent, Bali has experienced a rapid transition from an agrarian economy towards an urbanised tourist economy. Social changes included the massive inflow of Muslim immigrants from neighbouring islands, and the rise of a new Balinese middle-class. For them the village was a distant icon of "Balineseness" and the rapid growth of the modern economy and its global dimensions, a point of ongoing concern.

Protest

Since the early 1990s external investors have become more and more interested in participating in the tourist economy in Bali, and Governor Ida Bagus Oka (1988–98) proved to be a cooperative go-between, giving rise to the nickname Ida Bagus "O.K."[5] Growing feelings of discontent about the intrusion of Jakarta-based investors culminated in 1993 in the rise of a protest movement against the Bali Nirwana Resort in Tabanan, close to the holy sea temple of Tanah Lot.[6] The project was financed by the Bakrie group and included a five star hotel, condominiums, and a golf course, affecting in total 121 ha. of rice fields. Preparations started in 1991 and farmers received payments of Rupiah 2 to 5 million per *are* and were promised employment on the new resort. Despite the proximity to the temple of Tanah Lot the semi-government body Parisada Hindu Dharma raised no objections.[7] In November 1993, shortly after the water supply to the rice fields that were going to be converted into resort land had been cut off, the effects of the project were directly felt and a protest movement against the invasion of Jakarta's capitalism and its concomitant environmental damage emerged.

The protest movement consisted of a broad middle-class coalition of academics, public intellectuals, students, NGO activists, the regional newspaper *Bali Post* and representatives of the oppositional PDI (Indonesian Democratic Party). The rallying point of the movement was not ecological or anti-capitalist issues, but religious sentiments. It was the proximity of the resort to the temple that mobilised an island-wide protest that embarrassed both investors and government institutions. Religious arguments were instrumental in formulating a Balinese answer and mobilizing an alliance against unwanted outside intrusions.[8]

It was only after direct intervention by President Suharto, a warning by the military for the *Bali Post*, and a donation of Rp. 500 million from Bakrie to the Parisada Hindu Dharma that protest was silenced, and final consent was given to build a resort close to a holy place. Officially the Parisada decided in 1994 that no buildings were allowed within a distance of two kilometres from the temple, but this never materialised. In 1997 Le Meridien Nirwana Golf and Spa Resort advertised its soft opening.[9]

Commenting on the issue, the military commander in Bali, Maj. Gen. R. Adang Ruchiatna stated that "demonstrators are not part of Indonesian culture".[10] Public protest was indeed not part of the ideology of Indonesia's New Order, but it was now firmly positioned within a religiously informed Balinese discourse of discontent. This became evident when in 1997 another protest was launched against the building of a hotel at Padanggalak beach close to Denpasar. The issue at stake was similar to the Bali Nirwana Resort but the outcome was very different.[11]

In October 1997 the *Bali Post* reported that at the Padanggalak coast, which belongs to the village of Kesiman, a large tourist resort was being planned and that building activities had already begun without a proper environmental impact assessment. The owners of the project were based in Jakarta but the actual building was done by a local firm in which Governor Ida Bagus Oka was indirectly involved. The beach where the new resort was planned was an important religious site for the villagers of Kesiman and thousands of inhabitants of Denpasar where ritual cleansings (*melasti*) and post-cremation purifications were held.

As in the case of the Bali Nirwana Resort, the Parisada Hindu Dharma had already given its consent, and a broad coalition, this time also supported by local villagers, protested against the project.[12] In the village of Kesiman a powerful alliance was formed between villagers, customary (*adat*) leaders and the local nobility. They declared that the voice of the village *kulkul* (wooden alarm) would eventually be more powerful than government decisions. Resistance was coordinated by Anak Agung Kusuma Wardana, leader of the noble house of Kesiman who presented himself as a villager obliged to obey local customary rules and as a representative of the local nobility determined to defend his village against outside attacks. As a member of the ruling Golkar party, he occupied a seat in the regional parliament where he put the Padanggalak case on the agenda. Because Governor Ida Bagus Oka originated from the village of Kesiman, the village council decided to ostracise him (*kasepekang*). In terms of everyday life this had little impact, but in ritual terms it was a disaster with long lasting consequences. It meant that the village would boycott his cremation and prevent the proper continuation of the journey of his soul.

When he learned of the village edict, the governor immediately declared that nothing had actually been decided yet about the Padanggalak project, and that the village had, of course, a final say in this matter. With remarkable speed all building activities at Padanggalak beach were cancelled, and by the end of November 1997 the place had been restored to its former condition. Ida Bagus

Oka had decided to avoid a fatal confrontation with his village, which might have jeopardised the future well being of his soul as well as a future political career in Jakarta after his second term as governor ended in 1998. In May 1998 he became junior Minister and chairman of the National Family Planning Board in the new cabinet of President Habibie.

The Padanggalak case showed that a combination of middle-class protest and village-based resistance was strong enough to defeat a coalition of external investors and local administrators.

Hubris, Shock and Recovery

Despite protests against the boundless expansion of the tourist sector, the agony of growth prevailed. The change inspired Java-based Balinese sculptor I Nyoman Nuarta to design a 146 metre high bronze statue of the god Wisnu on the Garuda bird, the so-called Garuda Wisnu Kencana, which would become the highest statue in the world and the cultural marker of Bali, a symbol of ethnic pride and a non-Islamic identity. The project, which also included a theatre, restaurants, exhibition halls and a shopping mall, costs US$150 million, the majority of which was to be raised locally. The target date for completion was August 1995, when Indonesia celebrated the 50th anniversary of its independence. This goal was not met, and the new millennium was targeted as the new opening date. The monetary crisis of 1997 caused further delays and work actually came to a standstill. In 2003 only 15 per cent of the project had been realised. The giant upper part of Wisnu and the head of the Garuda were finished and had already become an object of veneration, but the building enclosure remained an empty space.[13]

The initial phase of the Garuda Wisnu Kencana project reflected a belief in an almost unlimited growth, and expressed a Balinese sense of hubris. While the 1997 monetary crisis (*krismon*) hit Java badly, the effects on Bali were less dramatic. Tourist arrivals in Bali were expected to reach seven million by 2007. Whereas the national economy contracted by 14 per cent in 1998, the Balinese economy went down by only 4 per cent. Recovery in Bali started in 1999 with 0.5 per cent growth and reached a level of 3.4 per cent growth in 2001. After the May riots of 1998 in Jakarta, Bali became a safe haven for mid-range Chinese businessmen, and the number of mini markets and internet cafes there increased. There were even ambitious plans to develop a Balinese "Silicon Valley" in the cool hills of Bedugul in the vicinity of the Executive Centre for Global Leadership and the 18-hole golf course of the Bali Handara Kosaido Country Club. A Balinese entrepreneur named Made Wiranata, owner of the Paddy Club in Legian, was about to launch his own Air Paradise, which opened direct flights to Australia.[14] With his brother Gede Wiranata, Made had started his career in the early 1980s in the construction business and expanded his activities into nightclubs, hotels, a taxi company, and textile production. Air Paradise started in February 2003, but ceased to operate in 2006.

The new governor of Bali, I Dewa Made Beratha (1998–2003), emphasised that Bali was a safe place amidst the turmoil of ethnic and religious violence in Indonesia. But he also recognised that Bali's tranquillity was fragile: "If a bomb explodes in Bali ... its image as well as Indonesia's in general will be completely ruined."[15] And he was right. The terrorist attack in Legian on 12 October 2002, one year, one month and one day after "9/11", shattered the image of Bali as an isolated safe haven.[16] Tourists immediately abandoned Bali and the recession in the tourist sector continued in 2003 owing to the SARS epidemic and the Iraq War. In the eyes of many Balinese the "Bali Bomb" marked a watershed. Before "Amrozi" (one of the perpetrators) things were good; after that moment, a crisis had erupted. The wages of about 40 per cent of the population declined, and thousands of people in the tourist sector lost their job. Parents were unable to pay school fees for their children, and the price of fuel, electricity, pesticides and fertilisers went up due to monetary measures taken by the government. The crisis trickled down to the streets of the villages, where daily earnings of *ojek* (motor taxi) drivers fell by 50 per cent, from Rp. 20,000 to 10,000 (approximately US$2 to 1).[17]

Balinese history is full of catastrophes and a sense of near disaster (or *kaliyuga*) is never far away. Since the late nineteenth century the island experienced an impressive series of crises:

Illustration 1: "Be careful our tourist sector is still......Aha promising!" (*Bali Post*, 9 October 2002, three days before the bomb attack.)

- 1880s–90s Internal warfare
- 1906–17 Colonial conquest, natural disasters
- 1930s Economic depression
- 1940s Japanese occupation and revolution
- 1950s and early 1960s Political tensions, volcano eruption, failed harvests
- 1965–66 Mass killings
- Since the late 1980s concerns about the effects of globalisation, ecological damage and uncontrolled investments
- Since the late 1990s political and economic crisis, terrorist attacks, impact of the SARS epidemic and the Iraq War.

In a period of 120 years there have been only three decades of relatively undisturbed prosperity, the period between 1919 and 1929, and 1970 through the late 1980s.

Such a history necessitates a strong belief in recovery as well. Remarkably there were no "revenge attacks" by Balinese on Muslim communities in Bali after the terrorist attack on Legian. Instead, a mass prayer for peace on 21 October 2002 marked a public effort to avoid ethnic and religious conflict. Psychiatrist and public intellectual Dr. Luh Ketut Suryani stated in the Bali Post (18 Oct. 2002) that the terrorist attack was a reminder of the gods that tourism in Bali had led to the loss of religious values. However, before the moral implications of the assault could be contemplated, immediate action was needed to stage a large ritual to release the souls of the victims and to cleanse the site of the attack from evil forces. An elaborate ritual, attended by thousands of people took place on Legian beach on 15 November.[18] It is generally believed in Bali that the early arrest of the perpetrators of the attack was due to this ritual. Such an understanding of divine intervention during the arrest of the perpetrators implied that the Balinese chief of police, Made Mangku Pastika, who received much praise in the foreign press, was merely an instrument of higher forces. Previous bomb attacks elsewhere in Indonesia remained unsolved, but the successful uncovering of the Jema'ah Islamiah network proved, according to this view, that Bali was different from the rest of Indonesia, and that Balinese culture was resilient enough to recover soon.

The ritual created some strains on relatives of the Australian victims, who wanted to commemorate the tragedy every year. Balinese, on their part, wondered why one should invite the souls of the deceased to return after they had been released with such care and splendour. For many Balinese, the ritual gathering in November 2002 marked the successful ending of the tragedy and opened the way for economic recovery and new flows of foreign visitors. Instead of commemorating the dead in October 2003, the Balinese organised first Kuta Karnival celebrating Bali's vitality. However, terrorist attacks in Kuta and Jimbaran on 1 October 2005 demonstrated the continuing vulnerability of Bali.[19]

New Rulers

The periods of prosperity mentioned above coincided with two eras of political stability under a strong state, Dutch colonial rule (1906–42) and the New Order regime (1966–98). Before 1906 the Balinese political system was fragmented, while during the period between

14

1945 and 1966 the weakness of, and cleavages within the central state reinforced patterns of conflict and economic decline in Bali.[20] With the end of authoritarian rule in 1998 and the ensuing wave of decentralisation and regional autonomy, the political pendulum seems to be swinging back towards fragmentation. I will discuss this pattern in greater detail below, but first I will look at changes within the administrative and political elite. In the next chapter I will deal with changes in hierarchical or caste relationships and the impact of decentralisation at the village level.

Reformasi came to Bali in the guise of numerous seminars and interactive radio talk shows, but brought little actual reform. Students from the academy of arts challenged the hegemony of the Balinese art establishment and accused prominent artists of collaboration with the New Order, but were not able to overturn the privileged position enjoyed by the group.[21]

Protest was also voiced against corrupt practices during the New Order period. Former Governor Ida Bagus Oka was accused of corruption and nepotism. In January 2001 he was even arrested and brought to court for misusing Rp. 2.3 billion of the Yayasan Bali Dwipa. In order to damage his reputation his opponents referred also to the role his father had played as a pro-Dutch policeman during the revolution. In April 2002 he was acquitted of all charges, but the executive director of this foundation was sentenced to one year imprisonment for the same case.[22]

Apart from these internal conflicts, there was a brief outburst of (anti-Islamic) "Bali Merdeka" (Independence for Bali) sentiment in October 1998 after Minister A.M. Sjaefuddin remarked in an interview with the Islamic newspaper *Republika* that Megawati Sukarnoputri was unsuitable as a presidential candidate because she had publicly worshipped at a Hindu temple. On 28 October 50,000 demonstrators in Denpasar demanded Sjaefuddin's resignation, but the minister remained in office. Another instance of anti-Islamic sentiments was the protest against a TV series aired by IndoSiar TV, which was situated in the eleventh century and portrayed, according to young Balinese intellectuals, Hinduism as an inferior religion.[23]

Anti-New Order sentiments manifested themselves in mass support for Megawati Sukarnoputri. In the early 1990s the oppositional PDI, forerunner of the PDI-P, had been relatively strong in Bali. In the elections of 1992 it won almost 20 per cent of the votes cast, but the number of seats the party held in provincial and district elected assemblies was modest compared to the comfortable majority of Golkar and the armed forces. The PDI gained in popularity when Megawati Sukarnoputri became party leader, but it was weakened in 1996 by an internal conflict manipulated by the government. Megawati lost her position and the PDI lost most of its popular support. During the elections of 1997 the PDI won just 3.5 per cent of the votes while Golkar and the armed forces monopolised power in the district assemblies. But when Megawati visited Bali in February and May 1997, mass demonstrations showed that she could still count on broad support among the population there. Because the provincial government feared demonstrations in favour of Megawati it banned the parade of so-called *ogoh-ogoh*, huge puppets of ogres during the night before Nyepi, or Balinese New Year, which could also be used to ridicule opponents.[24]

Megawati's strong position in Bali still was demonstrated at the first congress of the PDI-P (PDI's *reformasi*-era successor) held in Sanur in October 1998 when 50,000 supporters surrounded the Bali Beach hotel where the convention was held. There was "an outpouring of emotion and an explosion of energy", one witness wrote.[25] This atmosphere surfaced again during the elections in June 1999, which celebrated both the demise of the New Order and the victory of the PDI-P. The fact that the elections coincided with Galungan — the day when ancestors and gods descend — added to the euphoria.

Election Results in Bali

1971	Golkar	82.8	PNI	12.4
1992		78.5	PDI	19.7
1997		93.5	PDI	3.5
1999		10.5	PDI-P	79.5

The elections of 1999 caused a political earthquake in Bali. Golkar's share of the vote fell from 93.5 per cent to 10.5 per cent, while the PDI-P rose from 3.5 per cent to almost 80 per cent. The

PDI-P victory was primarily a manifestation of Balinese ethnicity, expressing anti-Javanese and anti-Muslim sentiments. These feelings erupted in a violent manner in October 1999 when it turned out that instead of Megawati, the Muslim leader Abdurrahman Wahid had been elected president of Indonesia. On the evening of 20 October and during the following day riots occurred in Negara (Jembrana), Singaraja, and Denpasar. Especially in Singaraja and Denpasar many government buildings were set on fire while the residences of the (Golkar) district heads were also attacked. The attacks were not a spontaneous expression of popular anger. Unidentified trucks coming from Java left a trail of damage in north Bali, while in Denpasar "unknown people" played a leading role in the riots, which ended as soon as Megawati was chosen vice-president on 21 October.[26]

Although the period between May 1998 and October 1999 did not bring fundamental reforms, there was a changing of the guard among the political and administrative elite. In 1998 Governor Ida Bagus Oka was replaced by the former provincial secretary I Dewa Made Beratha. Although not particularly reform-minded, he was an experienced Golkar bureaucrat and a skilful diplomat, who managed to accommodate an overwhelming PDI-P majority in the provincial parliament after the elections of 1999. Dewa Made Beratha had been a member of the provincial assembly from 1967–71, and caretaker district head of Bangli from 1968–70. In contrast to the previous governors who were assisted by military vice-governors (Dewa Gede Oka 1983–88, Aspar Aswin 1988–93, and Ahim Abdurahim, 1993–98), Dewa Made Beratha had two civil vice-governors, I Ketut Wijana and I G. Bagus Alit Putra, 1998–2003.

Number of Seats in Provincial and Regional Councils

Year	Total Number of Seats	Golkar	Armed Forces	PDI(-P)
1992	315	204	62	46
1997	335	249	67	8
1999	340	37	40	261

The provincial and district assemblies were controlled by PDI-P, and in contrast to other regions in Indonesia, where

17

experienced Golkar bureaucrats managed to retain their positions, in most districts in Bali new PDI-P leaders came to power. Apart from a shift from Golkar to PDI-P, the position of the nobility within the administration was also challenged. Until 2000 the majority of the district heads in Bali still belonged to the nobility, but by 2005 commoners prevailed.[27] In 1980 four district heads came from the military, two from the police and three from the bureaucracy; in 1990 two district heads came from the military, one from the police, three from the bureaucracy, and two from academic backgrounds. In 2004 the ruling elite of the Orde Baru had been replaced by a new group of district heads: four of them were entrepreneurs, two were politicians, one a dentist and one had a mixed background in education and the martial art *pencak silat*. Only two had bureaucratic backgrounds.

Background District Heads

	Nobility	Commoner	Javanese
1969	8	–	
1970	6	2	
1980	4	2	2
1990	5	3	
2000	5	4	
2005	3	6	

The demise of aristocratic rule was accentuated by the defeat of Bali's most famous royal lineage during the elections in Klungkung in 2003. The previous district heads had come from the royal house of Klungkung and maintained close connections with Golkar. New candidates from the *puri* tried to show a more progressive image by opting for an alliance with PDI-P, but despite support from the PDI-P headquarter in Jakarta, the aristocratic candidates were defeated by I Wayan Candra, a commoner who represented a new type of politician. A successful independent entrepreneur, I Wayan Candra was supported by the PDI-P at the grassroots level, and by various Pasek groups, large non-aristocratic kinship organisations.

He had mobilised both anti-Golkar and anti-aristocrat sentiments and ended the administrative rule of Bali's oldest dynasty.[28]

DPRD Bali	Seats	Non-Balinese	Nobility	Commoners
1971–76	40	7	17	16
1977–82	40	11	18	11
1982–87	40	10	22	8
1987–92	45	9	21	15
1997–99	45	8	12	25
1999–04	55	4	16	35

In general the fall of Golkar was accompanied by a decline of aristocratic power. The extent to which Golkar had been intertwined with the aristocracy is reflected in the composition of the provincial assembly. Especially in the mid-1980s Golkar hegemony coincided with a strong aristocratic dominance. In the 1990s, however, a gradual shift in favour of commoner representatives occurred. It seems as if it was no longer necessary for Golkar to rely on the nobility. Instead, the party had nurtured its own bureaucratic cadres most of whom were of commoner descent. A similar shift from nobility to commoners occurred also in the board of Golkar in Bali.

Year	Non-Balinese	Nobility	Commoner	Total
1972–74	5	5	3	13
1974–79	5	8	4	17
1979–84	3	11	8	22
1984–88	7	14	9	30
1988–98	6	13	15	34

This development was not unique for Bali. Michael Malley (1999) has shown that elsewhere in Indonesia Golkar started to rely more and more on its own regional cadres as well.

CHAPTER 3

Caste and Village

" C aste" and "village" were the two key concepts in colonial efforts to categorise, reorganise and control Balinese society.[1] In this respect we can trace interesting continuities: At the end of the twentieth century, *reformasi* manifested itself in Bali in terms of caste conflict, and after the turn of the century the provincial government issued a new regulation in order to strengthen the "traditional" village as the backbone of Balinese culture.

Changing Caste Relationships and Religious Reform

The sudden changes in hierarchical relationships that took place after 1999 accelerated a tendency that had become noticeable in the early 1990s. But that pattern has a much longer history as well. Leo Howe (2001) has pointed out that in pre-colonial times Brahman priests and noble rulers maintained an ambiguous relationship. Under Dutch colonial rule caste hierarchy was reinforced, but royal dynasties lost most of their power while the superior status of Brahmans was confirmed. Subsequently strong externally-imposed states have tended to reinforce caste hierarchy and especially the position of Brahmans, whereas periods of weak central authority (1945–66 and 1998–??) coincided with the emergence of egalitarian tendencies in Bali. Especially during the 1960s intercaste marriage became in this respect an issue of major contention.

Today's discourses about cultural and religious identities in Bali have their roots in the 1920s and 1930s, when a group of commoner intellectuals, who advocated a status system based on achievement and merit, challenged the aristocratic colonial elite who maintained that Balinese culture was based on caste hierarchy. The new intellectuals published their ideas in the journal *Surya Kanta*, while the conservatives voiced their opinions in *Bali Adnyana*. While both groups sought to achieve modernisation, representatives of the aristocracy emphasised the Balinese nature of their religion, which was rooted in *adat* and caste hierarchy, whereas their opponents pointed to the universal nature of modernist Hinduism, which was more egalitarian in nature.[2] Hierarchy would be contested or defended along these lines during the next 80 years.

Bali was also increasingly confronted by external challenges. On a political level the colonial state tried to counter nationalist influences from Java by emphasising a quasi non-political and static cultural authenticity of Bali.[3] In the field of religion the Balinese were confronted by Islam and Christianity, which challenged them to formulate what exactly their Hindu religion was about.

It was only in the late 1950s that Balinese Hinduism was recognised as one of the national religions in Indonesia. Initially Bali was considered as *belum beragama* (not yet having a religion), and Balinese had to prove that, if their belief was a religion, it had a god, prophets, a holy book and daily prayer. External criteria started to determine the parameters of religion in Bali and external allies and sources of inspiration helped to establish institutionalised Hinduism in Bali.

In 1958 Bali became a separate province and that same year Balinese Hinduism (Agama Hindu Bali) was recognised as a national religion. Two factors contributed to these developments. As a result of the creation of smaller administrative units Bali was separated from the neighbouring islands of Lombok and Sumbawa, which formed the new province of Nusa Tenggara Barat (NTB). NTB was dominated by the modernist Islamic party Masyumi, which was not interested in having too many Hindu Balinese within its provincial borders. President Sukarno, whose mother was Balinese, was about to ban the Masyumi because of its supposed involvement in regional rebellions, and was personally involved in the recognition of Balinese Hinduism. The step also reinforced Bali's international profile as an attractive tourist destination.

On the international level, Sukarno's efforts to strengthen the organisation of non-aligned countries, a body in which the Indian Prime Minister Nehru played a prominent role, created an opportunity for young Balinese intellectuals to visit India, where they were inspired by new modernist Hindu ideas.[4] Ida Bagus Mantra, who would become governor of Bali from 1978–88, was one of the first Balinese students who studied in India. Modernist ideas caused a gradual shift from ritualism to scripturalism, from magic to ethics, and from a collective to an individual experience of religion.[5] The emphasis on personal merit and individual daily prayers facilitated more egalitarian ideas in which achievement instead of birth determined one's position, while religion could be separated from caste.

The development of these new ideas became increasingly constrained by the rigid bureaucratic structures of the semi-government organisation, Parisada Hindu Dharma. Established in 1959 and initially intended as an anti-communist front, this body changed its name in 1964 to Parisada Hindu Dharma and became under the New Order a religious bureaucracy that was from 1968 onwards closely connected with Golkar. The Parisada was to a large extent modelled after Golkar, and its secretary general came from the armed forces. Intellectual life in Indonesia under Suharto underwent a process of provincialisation and a suffocation of critical creativity. As a result Hindu modernist ideas were gradually overshadowed by a bureaucratisation of Hinduism, expressed in an emphasis on religious regulations and ritual procedures.

Despite its intellectual poverty an important sociological change occurred within the Parisada. In 1986 Parisada was renamed Parisada Hindu Dharma Indonesia when it became a nationwide organisation with the task of supporting the "indonesianisation" of Hinduism.[6] The ongoing bureaucratisation of the organisation as well as its orientation towards "Hindu" communities outside Bali facilitated the rise of commoners within the ranks of Parisada. Like Golkar, which had become less dependent on the aristocracy, the bureaucratic structure of Parisada had offered commoners the possibility of challenging aristocratic dominance. This element was accentuated even more when the national headquarters of Parisada moved to Jakarta in 1996.

The rise of commoners within Parisada strengthened the influence of commoner groups organised along quasi clan lines, the largest of which is the Maha Gotra Pasek Sanak Pitu. Under the leadership of a former policeman named Ketut Subandi, who maintained close ties with Golkar, the group knit together diffuse local commoner groups such as Pasek, Pande and Bhujangga Waisnawa and newly invented kin groups, in an island-wide kinship network.[7] High on the agenda of these groups, or *warga* as they called themselves, was the recognition of their own priests at the same level as Brahman priests, or *pedanda*. Especially under colonial rule *pedanda* had secured a superior position *vis-à-vis warga* priests, who performed rituals at lower positions. Education and the rise of successful commoner entrepreneurs who were part of a new affluent middle-class, together with modernist Hinduism and a New Order discourse that at least in theory rejected the old caste system, stimulated commoner groups to demand equal rights and status for their own priests. Although the Parisada had already in 1968 acknowledged that in principle Brahman and *warga* priests were equal, in practice the Brahman priests still maintained hegemony over major rituals.

For many years protest movements against Jakarta took a religious form, but Bali's *reformasi* in 1999 took the shape of caste conflict and was focussed on one of the largest island-wide cleansing rituals, the so-called Panca Wali Krama, which would have its climax at the all-Bali temple of Besakih.[8] A massive alliance of commoner groups demanded that *warga* priests should act at the same level as Brahman *pedanda* giving rise to heated public debates and complex bureaucratic intrigues. Facing each other were conservative aristocrats supported by Golkar and Parisada leaders, and reform-minded intellectuals plus commoner organisations that threatened to boycott the ritual at Besakih. Governor Dewa Made Beratha helped the commoners to gain a victory, but conservative aristocrats were not yet defeated.

Caste conflict soon manifested itself within the Parisada Hindu Dharma Indonesia. Since the early 1990s Parisada had lost a great deal of its government subsidy as President Suharto started to support the newly established organisation of Muslim intellectuals, ICMI.[9] Meanwhile growing numbers of Muslim immigrants accentuated the "rise of Islam" in Bali. Alarmed by the invasion of both Muslim immigrants and Jakarta-based investors, and convinced of the need for a revitalisation of Balinese culture, Balinese intellectuals criticised Parisada for its lack of inspiration and inability to protect the Hindu community. Organisations such as the Forum Pemerhati Hindu Dharma Indonesia, in which public intellectuals like Prof. G. Ngurah Bagus and Ibu Gedong Oka and activists like Wayan Sudirta participated, and Forum Cendekiawan Hindu Indonesia, established as a response to ICMI, emphasised the spiritual poverty and loss of moral legitimacy of the Parisada. Faced with decreased government protection and external criticism, the aristocratic and bureaucratic power holders in Parisada had become vulnerable.

A Parisada congress held in 1996 in Surakarta, criticised the organisation for its intellectual poverty and emphasis on bureaucratic procedures. Jokingly it was said that the Parisada looked like *para seda*, deceased men. Attempts at this juncture to separate Parisada policy from Golkar interests and to increase the number of commoners on the board of the organisation failed.[10] However, during the next congress, held at the Hotel Radisson in Sanur in September 2001, the opposition succeeded in breaking down the Brahman hegemony within Parisada. The old board tried to turn the tide with the slogan "Parisada dengan paradigma baru" (Parisada with a new paradigm), a concept previously used by the TNI and Golkar in order to survive mounting criticism during *reformasi* and therefore associated with New Order conservatism. However, the newly elected board was dominated by commoners, and *warga* priests formed a majority on the advisory board. On top of that, a lay man was elected as president of the organisation, and this was a revolutionary development which was very hard for Brahman *pedanda* to accept.

While modernist Hindu ideas had gained ground in the national Parisada, a powerful group of conservative aristocratic dissidents in Bali remained loyal to old concepts of hierarchy, which they argued should be preserved in connection with Balinese *adat*. When these dissidents refused to obey the decisions of the new national board, Parisada in Bali split into two opposing factions, the so-called Parisada Campuan and Parisada Besakih. Campuan refers to the place near Ubud where in 1959 the Parisada had been established with army support. Besakih refers to the all-Bali temple situated on the highest mountain of the island and underscores the claim to represent all Balinese. Tensions ran high when in November 2001 the aristocratic opposition planned to hold its own convention and supporters of the national Parisada tried to prevent this and besieged the residence of the governor of Bali to force him to side with them in opposition to the aristocrats. The governor tried to remain neutral but many people suspected that he sympathised with the conservative Parisada Campuan. Interestingly only the regions, which were at that time headed by a representative of the nobility — Klungkung, Gianyar, Badung and Denpasar — supported the Parisada Campuan while the other districts backed the national Parisada, which held its convention in March 2002 at Besakih. Whereas Parisada Besakih criticised the "feudal" nature of caste differences, the Campuan group criticised the "Indianisation" policy of the modernists of the Parisada Besakih, which they claimed would eventually erase Balinese culture.

At the next conference of the national Parisada in 2002, in Mataram (Lombok), caste differences based on birth were once more rejected, and a liberal attitude was formulated regarding devotional groups like Sai Baba and Hare Krishna. It seemed as if the ideas advocated by *Surya Kanta* in the 1920s had eventually won the day, but the war is not over yet. An informal movement of radical commoners, called the Peguyuban Tiga Warga, aims to eliminate aristocratic participation in leading administrative positions. Their long-term strategy is to mobilise their constituencies in favour of commoner candidates once district administrators are directly elected. In 2005, however, this movement was weakened when its vocal leader, Made Kembar Kerepun, suddenly died.

The dissident Parisada Campuan can still count on substantial popular support as its chairman, Ida Pedanda Made Gunung, is a very popular public figure who has an influential talk show on

Bali TV. Moreover, many commoners are reluctant to give up their long-standing relationship with their Brahman priests. This can be illustrated by the dilemma of a Balinese friend of mine named Ketut. On the one hand Ketut as a Pasek should ask a Pasek priest to conduct rituals for his family. However, his family maintains a long-standing relationship with a family of Brahman priests. The breaking up of such a priest-follower relationship is unthinkable because it could bring illness and other disasters to the family and Ketut is not willing to take such risks. Moreover, Ketut likes to watch the TV talk shows hosted by Ida Pedanda Made Gunung, and he has concluded that in theory he is a proud Pasek, but in practice he prefers things to remain the way they are.

Hierarchical relationships have altered considerably during recent decades and change has accelerated since 1998, when caste conflicts became the centrepiece of *reformasi* in Bali. In conceptual terms the basic question was whether Hindu religion in Bali could be separated from culture and custom. Different external concepts introduced in the course of the twentieth century in Bali have led to fundamental changes in the way culture, religion and custom are represented as separate categories. Changes in the use of language suggest that social relationships tend to become more egalitarian as the capacity to use high Balinese has declined.[11] The Indonesian language is often used when people of different status groups interact in business and administration, because it offers a convenient neutral zone for wealthy superiors of low birth to address highborn employees. Also in matters of ritual there is a tendency towards a more egalitarian attitude. At the same time there is an increase of ritual activity. Modernist religious ideas advocate modest rituals, which enable more people to participate, and public transport has made it possible to visit virtually every temple all over Bali.[12] As a result Bali has become more Hindu than before, while religion is no longer exclusively framed in caste hierarchy.

Fragmented Autonomy: From *desa dinas* to *desa pakraman*

Parallel to the declining influence of Brahmans, the Balinese gentry, who dominated the southern rice plains in the pre-colonial period, also experienced a loss of power in the course of the twentieth century.[13] Initially the Dutch colonial government reinforced the power of the nobility at the local level by appointing many nobles as village heads. At the same time, however, the village replaced the *puri* — the noble house — as the basic administrative unit. Gradually commoners replaced members of the nobility as village heads, and in the course of time many noble houses experienced a decline in economic power and lost their dominant position as patron of the arts. Gamelan orchestras, for instance, were transferred to the villages. Eventually many noble families became members of the *banjar* — or hamlet — and recognised local customary rule.[14] Today in the sub-district in south Bali where I conducted my research, less than 20 per cent of the village heads are descendents of local *puri*, whereas in 1910, 90 per cent of the village heads were of noble descent.

In the 1930s Dutch colonial rule introduced a distinction between administrative (*dinas*) and customary (*adat*) rule at the village level. This construction was designed to keep Balinese religion and culture (*adat*) in a supposedly authentic state, while modern administration would form "a thin layer of modernity" touching village Bali only superficially. This *adat-dinas* divide was to survive well into the New Order, when the state penetrated deeper into village affairs and the *desa adat* was increasingly subordinated to the *desa dinas*. Various government regulations stipulated that *adat* was but an instrument in the pursuit of development and needed state guidance and supervision.[15] *Adat* remained, however, a contested field and on some occasions became a bastion of resistance against unwanted government intervention, as the Padanggalak case from 1997 illustrates.[16]

Reformasi and Law no. 22/1999 on decentralisation opened the way for a revision of the relationship between the *dinas* and *adat* spheres. Law 22/1999 abolished Law 5/1979, which had concentrated administrative power in the village in the hands of a small elite. Within village administration the old advisory board (LKMD) was replaced by a representative assembly (Dewan Perwakilan Desa) with representatives from each hamlet or *banjar*, and this body would control the village head.[17] However, in Law no. 32/2004, which replaced Law no. 22/1999, provisions regarding new democratic village councils were deleted.

It was not in the *dinas* sphere but in the *adat* domain where fundamental changes would take place. In 2001 the provincial government of Bali issued a regulation on the role of the *desa adat* (Perda no. 3/2001) that replaced a regulation (Perda 6/1986) in which *adat* was subordinated to the interests of national development. The new regulation reflects in many respects the concerns of urban middle-class Balinese who believe that Balinese culture should be protected against the evils of globalisation. Since Balinese culture is in their eyes rooted in the *desa*, and the *desa* is based on *adat*, it follows that *adat* forms the cornerstone of Balinese culture. In order to emphasise the authenticity and the autonomy of the traditional village, the word "*adat*", which was considered to be too colonial and too Islamic, was replaced by the term *pakraman* taken from ancient inscriptions of the tenth and eleventh centuries. The word *krama* referred to customary practice as well as the village council.[18]

Perda no. 3/2001 gives the *desa pakraman* full authority to run its internal affairs and makes the village council the highest authority. The *desa pakraman* has authority over village land, which may not be sold and is not subject to government taxation. Illustrating their newly acquired autonomy, some *desa pakraman* requested from the provincial government a larger profit from the tourist "objects", such as temples, located within their borders. Other villages even demanded money from nearby hotels for the view of an authentic village that their guests enjoyed. The new regulation also helped create opportunities for the *desa pakraman* to provide credit, set up local businesses and attract investors.[19]

Whereas under the New Order the *desa dinas* formed the main channel of government funding into the village, after decentralisation the provincial and district governments in Bali have preferred to subsidise the *desa pakraman*. In June 2001 the provincial government announced during a meeting in the temple of Besakih that it would donate to every *desa pakraman* a sum of Rp. 10 million along with a tax-free Honda Supra motorbike for the village head. According to the announcement, local *adat* had to be reinforced because "Bali was seriously ill."[20]

District governments also decided to support the *desa pakraman*. Law no. 34/1999 stipulates that ten per cent of the Hotel and Restaurant Tax has to be redistributed among the villages. In Bali these funds went to *desa pakraman*, but the distribution depended on regional wealth. Villages in the eastern region of Karangasem received in 2002 only Rp. 5 million per year, whereas villages in the rich tourist area of Badung were given 100 million each. Due to the effects of the "Bali bomb", income from tourism declined and in 2003 villages in Badung only received Rp. 50 million.

Officially Perda no. 3/2001 has been in force since March 2002, but its practical implementation remains uneven.[21] Although many Balinese dislike the new name, *desa pakraman*, they do appreciate the new flow of funds, which supports temple restoration and ritual activities and strengthens a sense of community.[22] However, a major problem is still not resolved, and that concerns the relationship between customary rule and national law. Customary rule, or *adat*, is ultimately subordinated to national law, which undermines the presumed autonomy of the *desa pakraman* in a fundamental way.

The Perda itself was also criticised. The first criticism concerned the position of migrants, and the second the quasi-republican image of the *desa pakraman*. According to the new regulation, migrants are members of the *desa pakraman* but they have no obligations to fulfil religious tasks. The same modernist ideas that separate caste from religion also differentiate religious and social spheres of interaction in the village. Hence, migrants are only expected to perform social and environmental duties, which are relatively light in comparison with the ongoing flow of religious obligations.[23]

In the second place the concept of *desa pakraman* was criticised because it ignores the many linkages that connect villagers with the outside world. It was based on a romantic desire for cultural authenticity mixed with Dutch colonial ideas about the autonomous and republican nature of the Balinese village, rather than a realistic appraisal of village society.[24] The consequence was that in Bali, decentralisation resulted in fragmented autonomy at the village level.

CHAPTER 4

Forms of Violence

In Bali the end of the Suharto regime did not lead to large scale violence between different ethnic or religious groups, but many villages experienced small outbreaks, often caused by local *adat* disputes. The rise of new political power holders was accompanied by the formation of militia that became allies with the political leaders within civil society. *"Adat"* was one way of framing violence, and cannot be separated from violence fuelled by the new political configuration. The emergence of a new "traditional" police in Bali illustrates how this process worked.

The Invention of Traditional Police Force

The new village autonomy was accompanied by the establishment of a traditional police force at the local level, the so-called *pecalang*. As early as 1996 and 1997 village policemen were active under this name in tourist centres of Sanur and Kuta. However, the place where this police force was truly launched was not in the traditional village but in the founding congress of PDI-P in Sanur, on October 1998, which was attended by thousands of people.[1] The armed forces were present with more than 3,000 men, but widespread suspicion that they were pro-Golkar and capable of causing riots instead of maintaining order, led to the PDI-P's organisation of its own security forces comprising of 1,200 men. The story goes that when tension ran high one man dressed in *adat* clothes managed to stop a crowd that was almost in a trance and persuaded them to sit down. The PDI-P congress proceeded in an orderly manner and it was clear that invisible (or *niskala*) forces, a concept deeply embedded in Balinese culture, had been at work here. Subsequently militias dressed in traditional attire have provided security for other big gatherings, such as the Bali Travel Mart in June 2000, and soon villages across the island started to establish their own groups of *pecalang*.

In June 2000 the provincial department of culture organised a seminar about the new phenomenon in an attempt to impose some uniformity, and in 2002 a booklet was published in cooperation with Parisada in which tasks, functions and dress of *pecalang* were explained.[2] Within less than four years a moment of charisma had been transformed into a new island-wide and village-based institution.[3]

Perda no. 3/2001 recognises *pecalang* as a "traditional" security force (*satgas keamanan tradisional*), especially with regard to *adat* and religion. Their uniform consists of a *destar* or head cloth, a flower behind one ear, a t-shirt on which the word "*pecalang*" and the name of their village is printed, a sleeveless safari jacket, a black and white chequered *kampuh* over a *sarong*, a *kris* that has been blessed in the temple, and a hand phone; tattoos are forbidden.[4] Thus attired, members are supposed to represent traditional authority, in contrast to the corrupt practices of an external and often absent police force.

Since *adat* was seen as the cornerstone of Balinese culture and the ultimate stronghold against the evils of globalisation, it follows that *pecalang* are viewed as the guardians of this culture. In a lucid essay, Degung Santikarma has argued that under the New Order, culture was conceptualised primarily in material terms.[5] As a commodity, culture could be reproduced and sold, but it could also be stolen, as was evidenced by a series of temple thefts in the mid 1990s that were attributed to "Javanese". It was therefore not only the task of *pecalang* to keep their village free from narcotics and other corrupting substances, but also to protect their territory from suspicious strangers.[6]

In most villages the new village policemen play a modest role,[7] although some have acted as well-paid and well-equipped security

Illustration 2: Sponsored traffic signs indicating a ritual
(photos by the author)

Illustration 3: Old and new village security guards
(*Bog Bog* 20, 2003)

guards, and others have become involved in criminal activities, the most visible — and often also rather annoying — manifestation of their authority is when they block entire roads and redirect traffic during temple ceremonies and other rituals, using commercially sponsored traffic signs.

Social Volcanoes

Far-reaching decentralisation, village autonomy and the establishment of a village police may have reflected the workings of democracy at the local level, but these developments also increased violent conflicts within and between villages. As regional autonomy grew, the coordinating powers of provincial and central government authorities have weakened. As a result, administrative institutions are no longer capable of managing many conflicts, some of which are long-lasting. Under the heading *"kasus adat"* — seen as a legitimate form of violence — land and border disputes as well as conflicts about caste and status claims within villages easily explode into violent action, often carried out by groups of unemployed youths. The Balinese journal *Sarad* has estimated that between 1997 and 2003 almost every month a *"kasus adat"* resulted in mass violence.[8] It seems as if villages have become less tolerant of deviant behaviour, and the implementation of social sanctions has become more violent.

> In July 2003 I Gede Kaler was burned to death when his house was set on fire by an angry crowd of villagers in the region of Karangasem in east Bali. Over the last 36 years the man had refused to obey *adat* rules in the village, arguing that he belonged actually to another village. Recently, however, he had inherited a plot of land in the village and this would make him a villager, but the rest of the villagers could not accept this and attacked his house. The relatives of the victim took refuge in a nearby police station, where they received temporary shelter. But it was not the police but local *adat* leaders who settled the case. Only after paying a fine of Rp. 500,000 to the *desa pakraman*, which was used to pay the necessary purification offerings, the family was allowed to bury the body of I Gede Kaler.[9]

Due to a combination of population growth, rising market prices for land, and the contested status of village land — private or communal — conflicting claims on land easily result in violent confrontation. According to Indonesian law the village is not a legal body, but villages do own land under local *adat*. In many disputes, conflicting parties refer either to national law or local *adat* to legitimise their claims.[10]

> In February 2004 an angry crowd of 2000 people from the village of Lemukih, fully dressed in *adat* clothes, threatened to attack the office of the district head of Buleleng, because the regional administration hesitated to make a decision about a prolonged land dispute in the village, which had recently surfaced again. It concerned 66 hectares of temple land, or *laba pura*, which were in the possession of 37 families who claim, on the basis of certificates, that they legally own the land. The village demanded however that the district head would invalidate the certificates. When efforts by the district head to reach a compromise failed, the 37 families received a social death sentence

(*kasepekang*) as they were excluded from ritual rights and obligations including access to the village cemetery.[11]

The case dates from 1930 when the 37 families received 96 hectares of land. In 1973 they agreed to return 30 ha. to the village. The district head had proposed that the 37 families would give a share of the harvest to the village, thereby recognising the village as owner but keeping the land in possession. Interestingly one of Bali's leading lawyers and human rights activists, Wayan Sudirta, supported the *adat* claims of the village. A somewhat similar case occurred in Culik in Karangasem:

> In 1985 the village had decided to build a school on land that belonged to the temple of a particular descent group comprising 130 families. Although initially the descent group had made no objections to the plans, after a while they refused to cooperate. When the group tried in 1992 to win their case in court they were socially expelled from the village. After an internal split 85 families of the descent group returned to the village. The remaining 45 families wanted to separate themselves from the village by establishing a village of their own. When their houses were set on fire in 1997 and 2002 by the villagers of Culik they took refuge to the provincial parliament of Bali in Denpasar. But even there they were attacked by people from Culik. Despite pleas by human rights activists the regional and provincial government were unable to solve this conflict.[12]

Apart from land disputes within the village, there have also been a growing number of confrontations between villages about conflicting claims on land and contested borderlines.

> In September 2003 large scale fighting occurred between the *desa pakraman* of Abianseka and Mas — both located in the administrative village of Mas, in the district of Gianyar — about the exact location of the border between the villages. During the attack people from Mas damaged an elementary school and the village temple of Abianseka while the administrative or *dinas* leaders of Mas had no power or authority to intervene.[13]

More parties were involved in a second conflict in Gianyar.

> This time the villages of Ketewel and Guang faced each other in a conflict over rice lands, which were gradually converted into real estate. Although the disputed plots of land belonged to the village of Guang, they were since the late nineteenth century possessed by

people from Ketewel who were followers from *puri* Ubud. The alliance between *puri* Ubud and Ketewel still exists, and has also a political dimension since both support Golkar. It follows that the people from Guang seek support from PDI-P.[14]

Although many "*kasus adat*" are new and have an economic background, others are rooted in caste conflicts or long histories of rivalries between villages, which tend to generate their own dynamics. Often caste conflicts within villages come to the surface when villagers boycott or even prevent cremations of aristocrats who have ignored local *adat* rules. Usually administrative and police officials are powerless in resolving these conflicts. Recently another old issue was back in the headlines of the local newspapers:

> In April 2004 twins of the opposite sex (*kembar buncing*) were born in a commoner family in northern Bali. Especially in the old days these children were believed to have committed incest in their mother's womb, and with their parents they were expelled from the village for a period of 42 days to avoid further pollution. The fact that this still happens caused a heated debate. Modernist Hindus considered this kind of "feudal" rules outdated and intolerable, whereas the village insisted to apply local *adat* rules.[15]

A typical example of warfare between two villages with its own historical dynamics is the conflict between the villages of Blahkiuh and Grana in the Badung region.

> The history of this conflict goes back to the early twentieth century when people from Blahkiuh migrated to the western part of the village of Grana some twenty kilometres to the north while they remained members of the *adat* village of Blahkiuh.[16] When during the revolution these "migrants" were denied access to the local cemetery guerrilla fighters from Blahkiuh had "settled the case". In 1972 hundreds of men from Blahkiuh had supported their fellow villagers in Grana when the original inhabitants from Grana had forbidden the migrants to take sandstone from the river. Led by one man on a motorbike a crowd from Blahkiuh — two trucks loaded with young men while the rest went by foot — had driven the original inhabitants off their houses into the rice fields. Access to the river was free again.
>
> In April 2002 the old conflict suddenly erupted again on the eve of Balinese New Year, or *Nyepi*. A few days before a volleyball match between the two camps in Grana was won by a team representing the "migrants", and it was believed that young men from the "original"

inhabitants sought revenge. They allegedly had already assembled stones from the river and provoked a conflict by disturbing a cleansing ritual in the hamlet of the "migrants". During the parade of the *ogoh-ogoh* (giant puppets), which is meant to demarcate village territory, youngsters from the two camps collided and started to throw torches at each other.[17] When a man from the "migrant" group was wounded, assistance was asked in Blahkiuh. As soon as the news reached Blahkiuh, the wooden alarm blocks were sounded and hundreds of men mobilized and left their houses. Although the local head of police and the *dinas* village leader tried to prevent an attack, the leader of the *desa pakraman* gave his blessing to help the fellow villagers in Grana. In trucks, cars and on motorbikes 300 men left within an hour. When they arrived in Grana, the "enemy" had already run away, whereupon they ruined the market building, a meeting hall, and the office of the local credit bank, while two cars, four motorbikes and a shop were burned as well. No one was hurt.

That same night a police force from Denpasar arrived but the men from Blahkiuh were not intimidated. They had done their duty and they had enjoyed their victorious raid. It had been great fun, even more so when they discovered that the internet edition of the *Jakarta Post* had published a report of the event: "We were world news!"[18]

The villagers of Blahkiuh were willing to sign an agreement, which should prevent outbreaks of violence in the future, but had no intention whatsoever to pay for the damage they had inflicted upon Grana. Once more, district administrators and police officers were powerless.

Increasingly, conflicts between villages, and between hamlets within the same village, are reinforced by political antagonisms. In most cases government administrators and the police are rather powerless.[19] Apart from the confrontations, which were reported in the media, countless near-conflicts occurred.

Meanwhile the government itself has also become the target of popular anger. At the local level police offices were prime targets of popular discontent. In July 2003 inhabitants of Abang (Karangasem) attacked the local police office after a thief had been arrested because they wanted to bring him to justice themselves.[20] In August and December 2003 police offices in Mayong and Jinengdalem (Buleleng) were attacked by an angry crowd because the police had tried to interfere in the election of village heads.[21] These attacks illustrate a lack of confidence among the population in the police.

Taken together, the long list of conflicts also demonstrates that the newly created *pecalang* were not able to prevent the regular outbreaks of violence at the local level. The extended process of decentralisation in Bali, which resulted in autonomy at the village level, was resulting in an administrative fragmentation that accelerated violent conflicts within and between villages.

What is still lacking in Bali is an overarching *adat* institution with enough legitimacy to solve sensitive *adat* conflicts and prevent outbreaks of violence. In the old days the royal centres were self-appointed "high courts". These institutions were replaced in the colonial period by regional courts, the so-called "Raad Kerta", but after independence these *adat* courts were discontinued because *adat* authority was gradually overshadowed by national law. However, national law never managed to gain enough legitimate authority to replace *adat* rules. The weakness of both national law and *adat* rules has in fact created structural insecurity in Indonesia.

In the 1980s Governor Ida Bagus Mantra tried to restore the legitimacy of *adat* by establishing advisory councils which played a rather patronising role, explaining to the people in a rather abstract way what their *adat* was actually about.[22] These councils were also expected to protect *adat* against the damaging influences of tourism. They organised competitions between *adat* villages, and in doing so pushed *adat* into the domain of folklore. Because *adat* had become imprisoned in the New Order developmental discourse it was denied to play an autonomous role.

Perda 3/2001 allows the establishment of coordinating *adat* councils at the (sub) district and the provincial level, but this did not materialise until February 2004 when the editor of the monthly journal *Sarad*, Ketut Sumarta, took the initiative to bring these bodies into being.[23] He was in particular concerned about land issues, and the unclear relationship between *adat* and *dinas*, which required a coordinated approach. However, in 2005 not much progress had been made owing to a lack of government support. It remains to be seen whether the newly-established councils are able to exert effective authority over local *adat* matters that are vehemently protected by local interest groups against outside intervention.

Sweeps

Another issue looming large over Balinese society and featuring high on the agenda of Ketut Sumarta's council was the influx of migrants and their position within local society. In the late 1990s what had been a steady flow of immigrants looking for jobs suddenly increased, as conflicts and crises drove people from Eastern Indonesia and Java to Bali. Most immigrants concentrated in South Bali, where they tried their luck in the tourist sector. The 2000 census counted about 250,000 Javanese and Madurese immigrants in Bali, out of a total population of 3.1 million people.[24] It is estimated that about 17 per cent of the population of Denpasar, or 200,000 people, are migrants while another 80,000 migrants live in the district of Badung. In some villages like Kuta and Sanur, Balinese are already outnumbered by migrants. Apart from a small group of well-to-do entrepreneurs, the majority of immigrants provide cheap labour in the construction and agrarian sectors, furniture and textile production, and in hotels and restaurants.[25]

In the mid-1990s anti-migrant sentiment erupted when holy objects were stolen from temples and Muslim migrants from Java were identified as the perpetrators. One day before the "Bali bomb" an article in the *Bali Post* asserted that every 1.5 hours a crime was committed by a migrant. Muslim migrants came to embody social pollution, which threatened Balinese culture. These feelings were eloquently summarised by the vice mayor of Denpasar in April 2002:

> Most of these people are jobless, they create a problem. They are criminals. There are problems with housing and traffic jams are getting worse. These people produce a lot of waste; they make slums.[26]

Although the terrorist assault on 12 October 2002 did not result in a violent cleansing of Muslims, the immigrant population of Bali did experience physical and administrative repression.

In the administrative sphere the municipal government of Denpasar took strong measures to reduce the number of migrants by applying an administrative "shock therapy". In order to obtain a migrant identity card (KIPP) migrants had to show letters from their home village as well as their employer and landlord in Bali.

The official costs of the card increased to Rp. 400,000 per year, to which a similar amount of bribes often had to be added.[27] In January 2003 the governor of Bali and the district heads reached an agreement to abide by one general rule, according to which non-Balinese migrants have to pay Rp. 200,000 per year for their permit, and migrants from within Bali only Rp. 20,000.[28]

The sudden rise in the costs of a permit temporarily discouraged people from moving to Bali, and it legitimised a series of razzias by government and village officials. Already in 1999 razzias had taken place, but after 12 October 2002 such measures were intensified. Immigrants who returned from Java after the fasting month were screened and intimidated by a combined force of regular police, administrative police and local *pecalang*. These forces also conducted razzias on a regular basis in Denpasar and other places in South Bali in search of illegal immigrants.

According to Perda 3/2001 non-Hindu migrants were not allowed to become members of the *desa pakraman*, which meant that they had no ritual obligations. This "privileged" position of migrants became a point of concern in many villages. During a meeting of *adat* village leaders in Gianyar early in 2004 emotions ran high about the supposed "take-over" of Bali by immigrants, and public intellectual Prof. Luh Ketut Suryani projected a gloomy future in which Hindu Balinese might become a minority on their own island.[29] Many villages put up signs forbidding "scavengers" from entering village territory, and *Nak Jawa* became a derogatory term for criminal strangers. *Pecalang* had the task of protecting their village — and by extension Balinese culture — against evil influences. They were depicted as vanguard troops, defending Balinese culture.[30]

In short, an answer to the threat posed by Western decadence and Islamic intrusions was found in the intimacy of the *desa pakraman*, but the "revival" of the *desa pakraman* and *adat*, with its conservative, male-biased and exclusive ethnic attitudes, is not in line with the requirements of national citizenship and democracy.[31] It is, moreover, difficult to determine the borderline between legal authority and legitimised violence on the one hand and the criminal activities on the other, of semi-official groups who act in the shadow of formal state institutions and political parties.

CHAPTER 5

Unstable Party Rule

F our factors increased political instability in Bali after 1998. First, the decentralisation laws no. 22 and 25 of 1999 stimulated district autonomy to such an extent that cooperation between districts at the provincial level was virtually absent, turning regional autonomy into administrative fragmentation. Secondly, in 1999 PDI-P had won the elections with an overwhelming majority but the new rulers had not yet secured full control over the bureaucracy, which was still by and large populated by Golkar (minded) officials, while new democratic rules also necessitated new relationships with local parliaments. In this context alliances between PDI-P and new militias emerged, which added a violent flavour to regional politics. In the third place, the sudden rise of the PDI-P caused a series of internal crises within local branches, and between local branches and party headquarters in Jakarta, which undermined administrative continuity at the district level. Finally national politics, and especially the elections of 2004, cast a shadow over Bali in 2003 as tensions between Golkar and PDI-P ran high.

Administrative Fragmentation

The relatively small province of Bali is — with its provincial administration, eight districts and one administrative town — rather over-administered. Since decentralisation has transferred funds and administrative tasks to the district level, the districts are often called "little kingdoms" and their leaders prefer to ignore the coordinating capacities of the provincial government. Although the old aristocracy has lost much of its former wealth and power and most regions are administered by commoners, the feuding factions at the regional level and the inability to cooperate at the provincial level remind many of the old days when various noble houses ruled Bali under the king of Klungkung, who was acknowledged as the highest authority but he was relatively powerless. Although in the early days of decentralisation some efforts were made to raise the issue of special autonomy for the province, the discussions did not produce concrete political decisions.[1]

Officials at the provincial level complain that they have more expertise on a variety of matters but are no longer consulted because inexperienced district administrations pursue their own policies. District heads often send low-ranking staff members to meetings convened by the governor about matters of common interest where he intends to arrive at a coordinated approach. As a result pressing problems concerning irrigation, the supply of drinking water, and a balanced development of tourism remain unresolved.

With regional autonomy, districts receive lump sums to finance their own administration and have more freedom to organise their own budget. The amount of money from the centre (*Dana Alokasi Umum*, DAU) forms in most districts, the bulk of the incoming funds. In 2002 DAU covered about two-thirds of Bali's total government income and two-thirds of the DAU was spent on salaries.[2] Many people in Bali believe that Jakarta should transfer more money to the island. According to economist Nyoman Erawan, Bali is entitled to more income from the tourist sector as a whole. Bali generates about 30 per cent of national tourist revenues, which are estimated at US$6.3 billion. Since 1 April 2004 most foreign tourists have paid US$25 for a visa upon arriving at Ngurah Rai airport in Bali, but these funds flow directly to various government offices in Jakarta.[3]

Although overall income has increased, expenditure has risen as well. While the 2001 budgets still showed a surplus, this evaporated in the following years due to "9/11", SARS, the Iraq war and the "Bali bomb".

A key issue in the relationship between the districts concerns a more equitable distribution of administrative funds and locally raised taxes. At the district level the amount of local taxes makes the difference. Eighty percent of the so-called Pendapatan Asli Daerah (PAD) is derived from the hotel and restaurant tax, Pajak Hotel Restoran (PHR). Already during the New Order, rich districts like Badung, Denpasar and, to a lesser extent, Gianyar generated large sums of money, while poor districts like Jembrana and Karangasem produced next to nothing in this respect. Although some adjustments were made to redistribute the PHR from the affluent tourist centres to less prosperous regions, major differences in wealth continued to exist and no structural changes occurred after decentralisation. Since the 1970s Badung was required to pay 30 per cent of its PHR and Denpasar 10 per cent to the other districts.[4] In 2002 the district assembly of Badung wanted to reduce its contribution to the other districts from 30 per cent to 15 per cent of the PHR. Governor Made Beratha needed all his diplomatic skills to reach a compromise. In July 2003 it was agreed that Badung would pay 22 per cent and Denpasar 10 per cent of their PHR to the other districts but not to Gianyar or to the provincial government.

Regional autonomy reinforced the tendency among districts to give priority to their own interests, and differences in wealth between regions did not decrease. At the same time there was an uneven distribution of funds between government sectors. As elsewhere in Indonesia, large sums of money went into prestigious new government offices, while, for instance, the educational sector was by and large neglected. Of the 27,500 classrooms in Bali, one-third needed urgent repair in 2003, and even the wealthy district of Badung had a shortage of 100 school teachers.[5] After decentralisation the district budgets show not only that differences in wealth between districts are maintained but also that Bali remains to a large extent financially dependent on Jakarta.

Preman and Party Politics

Apart from government, immigrants and ethnic conflict, other aspects of "Indonesia" have also reached Bali. The rise of PDI-P in Denpasar and Karangasem was accompanied by the formation of gangs of allied *preman* who provided public support in exchange for political protection and room to manoeuvre in the criminal sphere. I will focus on these developments in more detail, as they do not fit within the usual profile of Bali in the academic literature.

The genealogy of the biggest gang in Denpasar can be traced back to the 1970s when Ngurah P., a former leader of a PNI militia who had been involved in the killings of 1965, established the Armada Racun. This group wanted to protect Denpasar against the so-called "Anak Sudirman", or non-Balinese military from the Kodam (military command) Udayana, who tried to control the entertainment centres in Denpasar and Kuta. To secure protection from higher authorities the Armada allied itself in later years with the thuggish pro-Golkar youth group Pemuda Pancasila.

According to well-informed people in Denpasar, there is a direct link between the Armada Racun and the Forum Peduli Denpasar (FPD), which was established in September 2002.[6] Whereas the name Armada (army) Racun (poison) reflected aggression, the new Forum Peduli Denpasar (Forum Caring for Denpasar) presented itself in the guise of an NGO involved in a civil society discourse. With support from intellectuals, politicians, artists and entrepreneurs, the FPD stated in its "vision and mission" that it aimed to enhance the security and cultural unity of Denpasar and that it would fulfil this task in the spirit of the Puputan Badung — the heroic suicidal resistance of the king of Badung against the Dutch in September 1906. In his opening speech the chairman of the FPD, I Made Sutama Minggik, emphasised that the FDP advocated a bottom-up approach to development, resulting in a clean city, with fewer traffic jams where people would obey the rule of law. To reinforce regional culture, he promised to fight drugs and secular marriages.[7]

From the start the FPD maintained a special relationship with the mayor of Denpasar, Anak Agung Puspayoga, who acted as the patron of the organisation. Through him the FPD was also allied with the PDI-P and *puri* Satria, the old ruling dynasty of Denpasar. The leading ruler of Badung at the time of the Dutch conquest in

1906 was from *puri* Satria. In the 1930s and during the revolution *puri* Satria sided with nationalist forces while its main rival, *puri* Pamecutan allied itself with the Dutch. During the New Order *puri* Pamecutan was loyal to Golkar while *puri* Satria was a PDI stronghold.

Thus at first glance the FPD manifested itself as a decent organisation. It mobilised support for the refugees from East Timor, and offered assistance to the victims of the bomb assault in Legian in October 2002, for which they received a prestigious award from the national chief of police Dai Bachtiar during a big event at the Hotel Borobudur in Jakarta. However, the FPD showed a less friendly face when it attacked a defender of one of the perpetrators of the "Bali bomb" incident,[8] and the organisation was involved in anti-migrant sweeps in 2002 and 2003.

> In July 2003 the FPD operated as strongmen protecting the interests of their patron, mayor Puspayoga, when the group attacked one of his political opponents. When it appeared in July 2003 that the results of admission exams for high schools in Denpasar had been manipulated, as a result of which bright children were rejected and less talented children admitted, disappointed parents went to the city council to lodge a complaint because they held the mayor of Denpasar responsible for the fraud. They were supported by council member Trunajaya from PAN (Partai Amanat Nasional). When they arrived, the council was convening but the building was sealed off by police and a large group of FPD men dressed in black. When Trunajaya wanted to enter the building he was beaten up by FPD members after which a FPD gang destroyed the PAN office in Denpasar.
>
> Although the press covered the attack in detail, no one was arrested, allegedly because the police was unable to find witnesses who could identify the perpetrators. The chairman of FPD threatened to bring Trunajaya to court if he maintained his "slanderous accusation" that his organisation was involved in the incident.[9]

Commenting on this incident an academic from Universitas Udayana lamented that in the early days of *reformasi* he was often invited to participate in discussions convened by the mayor, "but now Puspayoga seems to rely on *preman* to solve his problems".

The FPD has its basis in the transport sector of Denpasar, and it controls entertainment areas and gambling spots. A closer look at the curriculum vitae of the chairman of the FPD, I Made

Sutama Minggik (b. 15 June 1952), reveals that his career is based on the connections between criminality, the transport sector and government.

> He did not finish primary school and started to work in the transport sector where he became a bus driver. He was also a member of the two most famous gangs in the 1970s, the Armada Racun (1973–75) and Suka Duka Pemuda Denpasar (1975–82), after which he established his own power basis at the Ubung bus terminal in Denpasar. As a driver he managed to get a job at the office of the governor and in 1968 he became a civil servant. Eventually he became chairman of the "Ngurah Rai" taxi cooperation and a member of the Golkar fraction in the provincial parliament. A timely shift to the new political leaders of PDI-P in Denpasar at the end of the 1990s offered him even more opportunities. Every inch a *preman* in his public persona, Sutama Minggik has based his power on his control of the Ubung bus terminal in Denpasar and various entertainment and gambling centres, from which he receives an estimated Rp. 125 million per month, which he shares with the police, and on his relationship with mayor Puspayoga, *puri* Satria and the PDI-P. The FPD functions in this respect as a formal NGO-like institution that harbours a variety of illegal activities, from which police, politicians and *preman* benefit.

The FPD is not the only gang in Denpasar. Its main competitor is the Laskar Bali, based at Jalan Iman Bonjol, which is led by Agung A., who belongs to the rival of *puri* Satria, *puri* Pamecutan. Where FPD is allied with PDI-P and the police, Laskar Bali maintains close relationships with Golkar and the army. Laskar Bali members also operate "upon request" to protect particular business interests. This happened for instance in May 2004 when they attacked people who wanted to re-occupy land in Pecatu, south of Denpasar, which had been confiscated by one of Tommy Suharto's companies.[10]

Alliances between the army and the Laskar Bali — and for that matter between police and the FPD — have not always been smooth. In November 2003 a fight occurred between members of Laskar Bali and some military in the karaoke bar Denpasar Moon. During the fight one soldier was killed and the military wanted revenge. Agung A. was arrested and remained in custody until he was brought to court in April 2004.[11] The judges did not reach a verdict, and in October 2004 the case was still lingering on because too many interests were involved.

Another murder case that attracted a great deal of public attention illustrates how old-style dynastic feuds became mixed with new political conflicts.[12]

In the afternoon of 11 November 2003 the leader of *puri* Pamecutan, Anak Agung Ngurah Manik Parasara killed his younger brother Anak Agung Putu Pranacita with a *kris*. The direct cause was a conflict over territory within the vast *puri* Pamecutan where many members of the old dynasty live. Younger brother Putu Pranacita objected to the decision of his older brother Manik Parasara to tear down a wall in the *puri*, and he did not recognize his older brother as the new, 11th leader of the dynasty of Pamecutan. The two brothers have different mothers; older brother Manik Parasara was of relatively low birth and his behaviour caused a lot of irritation among his siblings.

Younger brother Putu Pranacita showed his disloyalty towards his older brother by becoming a candidate for PDI-P running for a seat in the town council. As a result he allied himself with *puri* Satria and the FPD, and with fatal consequences.

After he had killed his younger brother Manik Parasara was arrested. In court he appeared in full *adat* dress and was accompanied by hundreds of followers.

Eventually the verdict was mild: six months in prison. But relationships within *puri* Pamecutan have not been restored as the murder has torn the dynasty apart. The leader of the Laskar Bali from *puri* Tegal, for instance, had sided with Putu Pranacita and was no longer willing to support Manik Parasara.

PDI-P in Power

Compared to Jakarta, Medan and other political hot spots in Indonesia, political violence in Bali is a relatively small-scale affair. But the cases mentioned here attract a lot of public attention and feature prominently in the political scene in contemporary Bali. The intertwining of administrative interests, party politics and criminal activities took place not only in Denpasar but also in the small town of Amlapura in the eastern district of Karangasem. Here the political influence of the local dynasty ceased to exist in the mid-1980s. After a period of military district heads, a new PDI-P politician, Drs. I Gede Sumantara, became the new administrator in 1999. He had a degree in public administration but more important was his network in martial arts (*pencak silat*) circles that helped him to win elections. Like the mayor of Denpasar, who could count on the support of the FPD, the new district head of Karangasem was supported by a "civil society" organisation, the Dewan Perwakilan Massa (DPM, Council Representing the Masses). The DPM is headed by Kari Subali, a tough guy with a big beard and a moustache, every inch a strong man, who can easily mobilise 200 to 300 men to underline the point he wants to make. He was also PDI-P representative in the regional council and member of the advisory board of PDI-P in Karangasem. Kari Subali supported his district head in a conflict with teachers who protested against job mutations. Together with a notorious criminal, Kadek O., who controls a large part of the illegal gambling business in Bali, he took action against the provincial board of the PDI-P in a conflict about a local branch of the party in the village of Rendang.[13]

As a new player in the political arena in Bali, PDI-P had a weak foundation in the administrative bureaucracy, which was still dominated by old Golkar networks, and the party had little experience in controlling decision-making processes in the district assemblies. Auxiliary forces like FPD and DPM were therefore helpful to support the interests of newly-elected administrators.

Apart from the marriage between party bosses and *preman*, the sudden rise to power of the PDI-P was accompanied by spectacular internal conflicts. In the districts of Jembrana and Buleleng *reformasi* and decentralisation offered ample opportunities for clever political entrepreneurs to seize power, while tensions between party headquarters in Jakarta and regional branches played an important role as well.

In August 2000 a new district head was elected in the Jembrana region of West Bali. With 17 out of 30 seats PDI-P dominated the district assembly and it seemed as if the party was in full control of the electoral process. The party candidate Ketut Sandiyasa had the blessing of the national headquarters and was expected to gain an easy victory. But due to a miscalculation he was unable to obtain the required 50 per cent plus one of the votes and a second round was needed.[14] To the astonishment of the PDI-P he was then defeated by an outsider, the dentist Dr Gede Winasa. Supported by a small fraction in the council Gede Winasa had made an alliance with Golkar, and managed to buy — as many believe — the votes of a majority of the assembly, including a number of PDI-P members.

Anger and frustration among PDI-P cadres led to violent attacks on the party office of Jembrana (ruined) and the house of the PDI-P chairman of the district assembly (burned), who was accused of treason.[15] The official inauguration of the new district head on 28 August 2000 ended in chaos and had to be postponed when a mob of angry PDI-P supporters of the defeated candidate Sandiyasa disturbed the ceremony. Several people were wounded and one man was killed. Eventually the formal inauguration took place on 15 November.

After his appointment as district head Gede Winasa became a member of PDI-P and in July 2003 he succeeded — against the wish of party headquarters — in gaining control over the regional branch of the PDI-P.[16] Local PDI-P branches decided to support Gede Winasa because he was district head. The election of Gede Winasa escaped the attention of the provincial leadership of PDI-P, which was deeply involved in the (re-) election of the governor of Bali at that time.

In November 2003 Gede Winasa finalized his quest for autocratic rule in Jembrana when he sidelined his deputy district head and appointed a new executive secretary who was a personal client.[17]

Despite his contested rise to power Gede Winasa achieved remarkable results as an administrator. Although Jembrana is known as a poor district, he managed to increase the local budget and provided both free education and free health services, so that the Indonesian weekly *Tempo* called him "a record breaking district head".[18]

Unstable party politics in Jembrana facilitated the rise of a new strong man who could use the PDI-P for his own interests. A similar but more complex process occurred in the northern district of Buleleng.[19]

In Buleleng the position of the district head I Ketut Wirata Sindu came increasingly under pressure after the elections of 1999. Wirata Sindu was an old and loyal Golkar administrator who had been active in the so-called "Golkarisation" campaign in Buleleng during the 1970s, which was intended to erase the grass roots support for the leftist wing of the nationalist PNI. In 1993 he had become district head and was now in his second term.

After the elections of 1999 PDI-P occupied 31 of the 45 seats in the district assembly and Wirata Sindu's room to manoeuvre was seriously restricted. He had to make deals with the leader of the PDI-P, I Nyoman S. Duniaji, whose star was rapidly rising in Buleleng. Nyoman Duniaji had been headmaster of a high school and a travel agent. While his father had been secretary of the Sukarno-era party PNI in Buleleng, he himself was a fierce supporter of Megawati Sukarnoputri when she was ousted from the PDI in 1996, and was actively involved in the establishment of the PDI-P in 1998. Supported by party headquarters and representing a new generation of reform-minded politicians, Nyoman Duniaji was in 1999 elected chairman of the district branch of PDI-P in Buleleng. In 2000 he became chairman of the district assembly (DPRD) of Buleleng, while a close friend of his, Dewa Kadek Astawa, succeeded him as chairman of the party branch.

The career of Nyoman Duniaji was resented by an older party cadre, Wayan Dangin, who had lost the elections for party leader and speaker of the district assembly. Wayan Dangin wanted revenge.

Meanwhile Nyoman Duniaji's power increased. As chairman of the assembly he made deals with district head Wirata Sindu, who depended on him for support. He organized overseas trips and cars for his fellow PDI-P assembly members and influenced decisions regarding infrastructural projects and the appointment of high-level officials. Towards the end of 2001 Nyoman Duniaji felt strong enough to start a campaign to replace district head Wirata Sindu. Ironically Wirata Sindu was supported by Wayan Dangin, who saw an opportunity to oppose Nyoman Duniaji's ambitions. But to no avail. In January 2002 district head Wirata Sindu was forced to step down, immediately after which Nyoman Duniaji started a campaign to be elected as the next district head of Buleleng.

Because Nyoman Dunaji was confident that he would win the elections, he started to ignore his local power basis. He rejected his political friend and ally Kadek Astawa (the local PDI-P chief) as running mate because he preferred a candidate with more education. Actually Nyoman Duniaji looked down upon most of his fellow PDI-P men in Buleleng and considered them backward and ignorant. Although supported by party headquarters in Jakarta, Nyoman Duniaji ran the risk of isolating himself.

Suddenly a new candidate appeared, Putu Bagiada, a businessman with a background in private banking in Jakarta. Putu Bagiada was warmly supported by Nyoman Duniaji's enemies, Wayan Dangin and Kadek Astawa. And as a businessman Putu Bagiada had ample funds to finance his campaign.

On May 7 the district assembly convened to elect a new district head. In his capacity as chairman of the assembly Nyoman Duniaji presided over the meeting. When he realised that he was losing the elections he tried to postpone the meeting halfway through the election procedure, but he failed. Putu Bagiaga was elected with 27 out of 45 votes.

Shocked by this unexpected defeat Nyoman Duniaji mobilized his supporters and staged demonstrations against the supposedly fraudulent election. However, in early July 2002 Putu Bagiada was officially inaugurated as district head, while Nyoman Duniaji remained a relatively powerless chairman of the district assembly. Ultimately Wayan Dangin had managed to defeat his enemy.

In July 2004, after the election of a new district assembly, Nyoman Duniaji's defeat was complete when he also lost his position as chairman of that assembly. An ironic twist in the Buleleng case, illuminating the flexibility of actors to engage in new alliances, is the fact that old enemies Nyoman Duniaji and Wayan Dangin closed ranks when they were both put in low positions on the list of candidates for the regional elections of 2004 by the newly appointed party boss of Buleleng, who wanted to get rid of the feuding factions.

In the end an alliance between old local party cadres with external money had defeated an alliance between a high-handed leader and party headquarters in Jakarta. Party headquarters was very unhappy with the fact that it had lost control over the party branches in Jembrana and Buleleng. In Buleleng party chairman Kadek Astawa was dismissed; he would later leave the PDI-P to try his luck in the small Partai Indonesia Baru. The other district heads in Bali were also worried by the outcome of the election and even decided to boycott the inaugural ceremony in July. The consequence of limited electoral democracy — i.e. restricted to district assemblies and fuelled by money politics — was that the PDI-P faced uncontrolled processes of infighting at the regional level of its organisation. Outsiders took the opportunity to penetrate into powerful positions, and this would also have serious repercussions for the election of the governor of Bali in July 2003, as I will explain in Chapter 7.

Rising Tensions

Campaigns for the national elections of 2004 started in Bali as early as July 2003 and caused violent confrontations between PDI-P and Golkar. Supported by its own militarised youth organisation, AMPG (Angkatan Muda Partai Golkar), Golkar made a modest but self-conscious comeback in the political arena after its devastating defeat in June 1999.[20] A rally staged in Ubud in July 2003, hosted by the leaders of *puri* Ubud and attended by party leader Akbar Tanjung, constituted a daring signal from Golkar that the party was back on track. Although the crowd was not as large as was hoped for, Golkar made an intimidating impression when a long and noisy "convoy" of vehicles circulated in and around Ubud before the meeting took place.[21]

In the aftermath of the event, tensions between PDI-P and Golkar and between PDI-P and its dissident offshoots increased in many places in Bali.

Two prominent leaders of the PDI-P happened to live in the village of Blahkiuh. These were the brothers Wayan A., who represented the party in the regional council of Badung, and Nengah U.M. who was the leader of the PDI-P in the provincial council. In 1999 they had enjoyed broad support from the population, which saw them as champions of democracy and reform. But things had changed. The two brothers had done very little for their constituency and people claimed that they had not kept their promises. While the two brothers prospered — Nengah U.M. had a free car and a salary of 30 million *Rupiah* per month — many of his old local comrades had the feeling that they were no longer seen to be of any use. One of their former strongmen in the neighbourhood said: "Since they are in power in Denpasar, they simply forget me. They are greedy because they refuse to share their benefits. Nengah U.M. had promised me his old car when he would succeed in becoming leader of the PDI-P faction. But nothing came of it. Look how they travel abroad, and how their "study visits"[22] to Hongkong and Australia are paid by the government. Useless! Oh boy, it will be hot during the elections next year!"

An effort by the local *adat* leaders of Blahkiuh to remind the brothers of their responsibilities back home by appointing them as *pecalang* (*adat* policemen) in the village failed. When they joined a group of *pecalang* on the eve of Balinese New year in 2002 they were yelled at and told to go home.

Gradually the hamlet where the brothers live shifted its loyalties and started to support Golkar. As a result, the red PDI-P banner in the yard of the two bothers faced a huge yellow banner on the other side of the road, reminding them that they were loosing ground within their own community.

Tensions between Golkar and PDI-P erupted briefly during a soccer match between the team of the hamlet where the brothers live, which was rapidly moving towards Golkar, and a team from a neighbouring hamlet where people still supported PDI-P. A small incident soon erupted into a big fight. The match was immediately halted, and only due to direct intervention by the village leaders, violence did not spread.[23]

Similar incidents occurred elsewhere. Especially in Tabanan, Jembrana and Buleleng numerous small incidents were reported, such as the tearing and burning of banners belonging to opposing parties and occasionally attacks on party *posko* (*pos komando*) and offices.[24] Towards the end of October tensions increased when Golkar planned to hold its 40th anniversary in Bali, and PDI-P announced it would celebrate the national commemoration of the 1928 "Youth Oath" with large parades and other manifestations. On Sunday 26 October 2003, a PDI-P parade near Singaraja in Buleleng was attacked by Golkar supporters. Not long afterwards a PDI-P mob retaliated and lynched two members of the youth organisation of Golkar in the village of Petandakan. Violence continued during the next two days around Singaraja and consisted mainly of attacks on Golkar offices.[25]

These incidents caused a great deal of concern among party leaders in Jakarta. If events in Bali and elsewhere were to set the tone for the national elections, what would happen in other parts of Indonesia? Both government officials and party bosses put pressure on the local branches of their parties in Bali to refrain from further violence. They succeeded, but many people feared that violence might flare up when the real campaign of the elections of April 2004 got underway.

Violence between parties was replaced by internal conflicts about the ranking order of candidates for the regional elections, which were also held in April 2004. In November 2003 in Badung, Karangasem and Tabanan angry supporters of frustrated candidates, who got a low ranking, attacked party offices and burned party banners.[26] After the incidents in Buleleng, local Golkar cadres, led by former policeman and local thug I Ketut Sadia, who were disappointed by the lack of support they had received from their national leaders, left the party and established an independent militia, called Garda Buleleng. Following the model of the FPD in Denpasar they sought support from district head Putu Bagiada.

These events confirm the correlation between the weak central state and political fragmentation at the provincial level described by Geoffrey Robinson (1995) for earlier periods of Balinese history.

CHAPTER 6

Ajeg Bali

Lack of administrative coordination, violent *adat* cases, internal party turmoil, confrontations between political parties, immigrants, *preman* and other Indonesian phenomena provide a clear illustration that the old dichotomy between an isolated Bali and its fragile culture on the one hand, and the evils of the outside world on the other, no longer holds true. Bali has of course always been open to outside influences, and has from the beginning been an integral part of the Indonesian nation-state. But since regional autonomy was set in motion the artificial moral dichotomy between an innocent Bali and an evil outside world was difficult to maintain. It can no longer be denied that "evil" is now a palpable presence in Bali itself.[1] However, within Bali the main sources of evil were still located in the outside world: globalisation and, after the bomb blast in Legian, international terrorism. The threat of globalisation — in the guise of a free movement of trade, capital and labour as well as the demoralising impact of drugs and decadence — has motivated concerned urban intellectuals to participate in countless seminars where they discuss these phenomena in the context of regional autonomy.[2] A revealing example of these gatherings was a prestigious symposium held in July 2000 on cultural heritage conservation, sponsored by the World Bank and UNESCO. Here old discourses about the uniqueness of Bali (commonplace since the nineteenth century) and efforts to preserve Balinese culture (since the 1920s) resurfaced in empty "newspeak". Since the uniqueness of Bali, its environment and cultural traditions were under challenge, the recipe for sustained development should consist of "the empowerment of governance of local communities", "the revitalisation of historic towns", and "the adaptation of tradition and the renewal of the cultural fabric by keeping living cultural practices alive".[3] It was along these lines that "Balinese move into the future by returning to their past, and embrace modernity by re-acquainting themselves with old traditions", as Leo Howe observed.[4] This approach is both inward-looking and conservative.

It was in this context that the new leader of the independent Bali Post Group, Satria Naradha, launched his *Ajeg* Bali campaign in 2002. The son and heir of Ketut Nadha, founder of the *Bali Post* in 1948 and its chief editor until his death in 2001, Satria Naradha became the self-appointed leader of a moral middle-class movement that claimed to protect and strengthen Balinese culture.[5]

During the late 1990s and especially under Satria Naradha the *Bali Post* became a powerful provincial media concern, which now includes a local TV station, four radio stations, the well-respected *Bali Post* newspaper itself, the daily *Denpost* that mainly covers criminality, and several other newspapers and magazines. Although the Bali Post Group has no monopoly — *Jawa Pos* with its imprint *Radar Bali*, the newspaper *NUSA*, and commercial television stations are alternative sources of news[6] — Satria Naradha is well-equipped to shape the political agenda. If necessary, he is willing to impose censorship.

In an interview in June 2004 Satria Naradha claimed that he received his inspiration to launch the concept of "*Ajeg* Bali" as early as the 1980s, when he was still a high school pupil. "When I was meditating I received the idea, but I could not yet give it a name, but when in the 1990s I saw large billboards mobilising people to safeguard Bali, I suddenly knew what it should be." Others think that the modernist Muslim and Hindu movements of the 1990s, when Satria Naradha was studying journalism in Surabaya, were an important inspiration for his later activities as a cultural activist.[7] Satria Naradha's ideas also fit within a discourse on cultural preservation in Bali that was already initiated in the 1990s.

"*Ajeg* Bali" was launched at the opening of Bali TV in May 2002, when the governor of Bali, I Dewa Made Beratha urged his audience to *mengajegkan* Balinese *adat* and culture.[8] The word *"Ajeg"* carries the meaning of strong, upright, and is in a way a stronger version of the notion of *"kebalian"*, or "Balineseness", which was previously used in a similar way. Related terms like *ajeg-ajeg* and *ajegang* refer to village regulations and locate the term in the centre of Balinese culture.[9] The notion of *"ajeg"* is a loose category that offers different groups of people a comfortable way to talk about Bali. Although some of my middle-class intellectual friends dislike the conservative tone of the *Bali Post*, the dull programmes shown on Bali TV, and the post-New Order nature of the *Ajeg* Bali discourse, many ordinary Balinese like the concept:

- *"Ajeg* means that we should go back to the origins. Back to the pure and peaceful Bali, when things were orderly and true."
- *"Ajeg* means that Bali is safe and can resist terrorists."
- *"Ajeg* Bali offers us an answer to modernization without substance."

They also like the way *Ajeg* Bali is communicated on local television. News and the prime time horror show *Sekala dan Niskala* address familiar topics, and Balinese soap operas offer a welcome alternative to the Jakarta-based *"sinetron"* situated in an air-conditioned upper class world largely unfamiliar to many Balinese. Although the rather folkloristic formats of talk shows on Bali TV seem clumsy, and guests are expected to appear in full *adat* dress, the messages have an impact. Especially in the talk show *"Ajeg* Bali" Balinese culture is presented as homogeneous and relatively static, something essentially religious and rooted in village *adat*.

Balinese culture is also increasingly presented as exclusively Hindu. This is achieved by emphasising contrasts with Islam and, ironically, by imitating Islamic styles. In contrast to the Islamic salutation *Assalam'alaikum*, anchormen, reporters and talk show hosts start with a solemn *Om Swastiastu*, and conclude with *Om Shanti Shanti Om*, while they bring their hands together in front of their face.[10] When most national networks broadcast the Islamic evening prayer (*adzan magrib*), Bali TV broadcasts a Hindu prayer (*puja trisandya*) at six o'clock that follows the Islamic format and uses phrases derived from a Protestant style of prayers. There is even a discussion whether Hindu Balinese should have their own version of *halal* (allowed) and *haram* (not allowed) food. A televised series of 285 episodes of a drama imported from India reminds the Balinese that they are part of a huge civilisation that is much older than Islam.

One of the most popular programmes in Bali is the talk show *Dharma Wacana* (sponsored by Toyota) which was till 2006 daily on air. The presenter is Ida Pedanda Made Gunung — chairman of the conservative Parisada Campuan — who discusses religious topics and their practical moral implications. He is a witty man and his audience often laughs about the points he makes. Although he is not openly hostile to immigrants, the following message is clear enough: "Many Balinese sell their land in order to eat lots of *sate* (grilled meat), but don't forget that many immigrants sell *sate* in order to buy a lot of land."

> *Dharma Wacana* is a recording of talks given by Pedanda Made Gunung during his visits to numerous temples all over Bali. At 28 August 2005 he visited the Pura Panataran Agung of Blahkiuh, an occasion that was considered a major event by the villagers. People not only felt honoured by the visit of this famous priest but they also looked forward to enjoying his witty performance. At 4 o'clock in the afternoon the front yard of the temple was crowded and for the next two hours three hundred people listened to an uninterrupted flow of words.
>
> Sitting behind his laptop, Pedanda Made Gunung addressed a series of issues — the dangers of decadence, cock fights, alcohol and drugs, the importance of religious knowledge, the relationship between man and nature, and, of course, *Ajeg* Bali. His approach was to introduce an abstract religious concept, give some examples from everyday life mixed with one or two jokes, and finally conclude the topic with a moral lesson. His basic message was that people should live a modest decent life in balance with nature, and that *Ajeg* Bali should be seen in terms of maintaining a fixed identity grounded in the sacredness of Bali.

The power of Pedanda Made Gunung's performance lay in the way he combined abstract notions and everyday concerns, and phrased his messages in an accessible and entertaining way. Pedanda Made Gunung's interpretation of *Ajeg* Bali represents a conservative romanticism: the goodness of Bali is rooted in village values, while evil comes from the outside. His teachings also reflect the Hindu curriculum from the New Order that emphasised a territorial-based order and balance. Although his performance suggests that he identifies himself with ordinary people and favours a more egalitarian society, he actually strongly supports the maintenance of caste hierarchy.[11] According to him, Brahmans are the trees in whose shade Balinese society will prosper while it is defended by the Satria nobility.

Although many public intellectuals support the notion of *Ajeg* Bali, a minority have criticised the top-down character of the campaign, comparing it with the compulsory Pancasila courses of the New Order period. They fear that *Ajeg* Bali, because of its vagueness, could be used to silence critical voices, and the magazine *Sarad* has warned against the return of "feudal" attitudes.[12] Degung Santikarma has remarked in this respect that *Ajeg* Bali was developed by bureaucrats and supported by middle-class people who have an interest in the tourist sector. Where an older notion of cultural conservation represented Bali as a vulnerable woman who needed protection from a strong state, *Ajeg* Bali depicts Balinese culture in much more aggressive male terms, ready to face and resist the outside world.[13] Despite these criticisms the *Ajeg* Bali discourse has gained ground in a short period of time, becoming a successful brand name for a new cultural consciousness with important political implications.[14]

Satria Naradha's prime intention was to unify Bali through his *Ajeg* Bali campaign. His political agenda focussed on various issues. He was anxious to prevent the spread of political violence, and in September 2003 organised a seminar on the small-scale warfare between political parties while the *Bali Post* published a series of critical articles.[15] He was also concerned about the absence of administrative coordination in Bali and urged district heads to cooperate more closely with the governor. At the launch of Bali TV he invited these administrators to hold one torch together, symbolising the unity of Bali. To gain support and legitimacy for his campaign, Satria Naradha invited administrators and high-ranking guests to sign so-called *prasasti*, stone inscriptions through

**Illustration 4: The sultan of Jogjakarta signing a *prasasti*
while Satria Naradha stands in the background**
(*Bali Post*, 14 Sept. 2003)

which they endorse the intentions of *Ajeg* Bali. In doing so he
"revived" an ancient royal tradition of issuing stone inscriptions and
continued a New Order habit of commemorating official events
with an inscribed signature of a state authority. Interestingly, these
prasasti were all written in Balinese script, but the language rendered
into that was Indonesian! All senior administrators of Bali, national
politicians and the sultan of Jogjakarta have signed *prasasti*, which
are gathered in the *Bali Post* headquarters.

In January 2005 Satria Naradha proclaimed ten *"Ajeg* Bali
Heroes", while the *Ajeg* Bali campaign targeted schools and became
part of the curriculum, including competitions for the best *ajeg*
teacher, *ajeg* pupil, *ajeg* performance, *ajeg* prayer etc.[16] In addition to
the standardisation of praying styles and ritual practices, *ajeg* Bali also
affects dress codes. For most ceremonies people are expected to wear
white, but for cremations they are advised to dress in black. Besides
standardisation, there occurs, according to Elisabeth Rhodes (2007),
also a process of sanitation. "Inhumane" aspects, such as animal
sacrifice, cock fighting and tooth filing are discouraged. Meanwhile,
the term *"Ajeg"* appeared almost everywhere, in newspaper articles,
on banners during public meetings, and in casual *"warung* talk".[17]

The *Ajeg* Bali campaign has been instrumental in emphasising an exclusive ethnic profile of Balinese culture and religion. Ethnic unity is in turn based on religion. Bali's police chief Mangku Pastika stated in this respect that "Ajeg Bali has to be Ajeg Hindu."[18] When I met Satria Naradha in 2005 he talked about *Ajeg* Bali in terms of a "cultural renaissance", but when my assistant asked him casually what this meant in practice he immediately put the sweeping of immigrants on top of the agenda. Number two on the list was a demand for more Balinese in the next government, and number three a plea for special autonomy for the province of Bali. In another context he said that he wanted a confrontation with the migrants. The idea that the main threat to Bali is embodied by immigrants is widely shared by urban intellectuals.[19]

To push immigrants out of the informal sector, Satria Naradha established the "Kooperasi Krama Bali". Only native Balinese — who can prove that they are member of a village — may become a member of this cooperative, which supports small entrepreneurs. In the district of Gianyar, foodstalls selling "original Balinese noodles" — which are supposed to be made from pork meat — were set up by this cooperative. Through a clever public relations campaign, political leaders, administrators and other public figures were persuaded to support this cooperative. Moreover, the son of the governor was appointed as the secretary of the cooperative, sealing the alliance between government, *Bali Post* and the *Ajeg* Bali campaign. Commenting on the political influence of Satria Naradha some people even wondered in this context whether Bali has actually *two* governors. Recently, there is much speculation in Bali about Satria Naradha's ambitions to become governor.

Despite its flexible vagueness, *Ajeg* Bali has a rigid ethnic and religious agenda. Since the position of the aristocracy has been weakened and caste hierarchy is contested, *Ajeg* Bali offers urban intellectuals and middle-class officials an opportunity to represent Bali as a homogeneous culture able to face external threats. At the same time the *Ajeg* Bali discourse erases conflicts concerning class, caste, religion and ethnicity, while legitimising violence (by *pecalang*) in the name of culture.

CHAPTER 7

Elections

Beginning in 1999 a series of democratic elections were held in Indonesia — in 1999 and 2004 for the national parliament and district and provincial assemblies, and in 2004 also for the presidency; in 2005 in a large number of districts new district heads were elected. Electoral democracy has taken root in Bali but important changes in the nature of these elections can be identified as well. The elections of 1999 celebrated the victory of Megawati's PDI-P, but the gubernatorial elections of 2003 marked a serious crisis within the PDI-P, as a result of which support for Megawati dwindled during national elections of 2004. Finally, during the district elections of 2005 the hegemony of political parties was seriously challenged by the emergence of new independent local leaders.

· 2003: Gubernatorial Elections and *Ajeg* Bali

The connections between the *Bali Post*, politics and the *Ajeg* Bali campaign became visible during the campaign leading to the re-election of Governor Dewa Made Beratha in August 2003. The election showed how party politics and media interests were closely intertwined and how the *Ajeg* Bali campaign was used to cover up corruption within the PDI-P.

The election of the governor needs to be seen within a broader context of national politics. President Megawati and her PDI-P sought to strengthen support among governors and district administrators, who were expected to help her win the presidential elections of 2004. In a series of controversial elections — in Jakarta, Lampung, Central Java and East Java — local PDI-P candidates were ignored in favour of strong "non-cadre" favourites of party headquarters in Jakarta. Alerted by the stubbornness of local party branches in Buleleng and Jembrana, PDI-P leaders in Jakarta approached the provincial leaders of the party in May 2003 to "synchronise" the strategy for the upcoming election of the governor of Bali.[1] It turned out that party headquarters preferred the re-election of Governor Dewa Made Beratha and rejected the local PDI-P candidate Cokorda Ratmadi. Ratmadi was district head of Badung while his brother, Anak Agung Puspayoga, was mayor of Denpasar. Both came from *puri* Satria Denpasar, an old and respected PNI/PDI(-P) stronghold. Megawati preferred Made Beratha, who had a Golkar background, because he had facilitated the founding PDI-P congress in Bali in October 1998, a move that now turned out to have been a timely political investment of his. Megawati counted on the loyalty of "her" people in Bali and tried to gain extra support in Golkar circles by choosing Made Beratha. This was a serious miscalculation.

When rumours leaked out in May 2003 that PDI-P headquarters did not support the local candidate, panic spread in party circles in Bali. In late June all PDI-P members of the provincial assembly were invited to Jakarta where they were told to support Megawati's candidate. For the time being the provincial PDI-P decided to support two candidates: Cokorda Ratmadi *and* Dewa Beratha.[2] On 21 July party headquarters instructed the provincial PDI-P to drop the candidacy of Cokorda Ratmadi and to vote for Made Beratha. This order caused a revolt among party cadres, who screamed that the ideals of the party were crushed and that it was now an all-out fight between them and Jakarta.[3] Three days later Megawati visited Bali for an international meeting of the ASEM countries. She met Cokorda Ratmadi briefly and told him: "If you want to disgrace me, go ahead." The same day riots broke out in Semarang when Megawati's favourite was elected as governor of Central Java, defeating the local PDI-P candidate.[4]

In Bali emotions ran high, confusing conflicts erupted over procedures — who was actually entitled to speak on behalf of PDI-P headquarters, the letter from Jakarta arrived after the deadline to nominate candidates, and so on — and pressure on Cokorda Ratmadi increased. Eventually on Monday 28 July Ratmadi announced in front of weeping supporters that he had withdrawn his candidacy.

From then on, the *Bali Post* played an active role as a reconciling mediator. Instead of presenting Cokorda Ratmadi's withdrawal as a defeat, the newspaper praised him as "*Sang Pahlawan Ajeg Bali*", the Hero of a Strong and Unified Bali, who had sacrificed his personal interests to serve a higher public cause. In order to emphasise harmony, Satria Naradha staged on August 2 a reconciliation ceremony in *puri* Satria, which was directly broadcasted on Bali TV and received front page coverage in the *Bali Post*.[5] Reconciliation was underlined by the signing of yet another *prasasti*, which symbolised the peace between Made Beratha and *puri* Satria and the pledge of all parties to support *Ajeg* Bali. Demonstrations by PDI-P supporters against Dewa Made Beratha, which took place away from the cameras, were not mentioned, and no large scale riots occurred.

Although the owner of the *Bali Post*, Satria Naradha, had been close to *puri* Satria, he had his own reasons for supporting Made Beratha. His television station was in jeopardy because it had started broadcasting before the new law on local television (Law no. 32/2002) was in operation. Strictly speaking, Bali TV was illegal, and Jakarta could close the station down. Satria Naradha needed Made Beratha's mediation in Jakarta to stay on the air, and his play eventually succeeded.

The role played by the *Bali Post* in this matter shows that the local press is not always the best agency to reveal background information about local conflicts and other sensitive issues. In fact the mass media may become involved as interested parties, either by taking sides, or by playing an active role of their own.

After the withdrawal of Cokorda Ratmadi and the public reconciliation in *puri* Satria, it seemed as if most of the tension was over. In August 2003 the PDI-P members of the provincial

Illustration 5: Cokorda Ratmadi and *Ajeg* Bali
(*Bali Post*, 30 July 2003)

assembly made a pilgrimage to the temple of Besakih and the
next day they were locked up (*dikarantina*, quarantined) in Hotel
Bali Cliff, where they would remain until the election of the new
governor on 6 August.[6] Dewa Made Beratha was re-elected with
31 votes (out of 55 assembly members), which was reported by the
Bali Post as a "victory of *Ajeg* Bali".[7]

Meanwhile other media revealed that bribery had occurred on
a large scale shortly before the election.[8] Two PDI-P members
had confessed to receiving Rp. 50 million (US$5,000) from a
representative of PDI-P headquarters, who had visited them in
Hotel Bali Cliff. Another amount of Rp. 100 million (US$10,000)
would be transferred after the election. For its part, the *Bali Post*
only reported that allegations about bribery had been denied by
provincial party leaders.[9] The fact that Bali Corruption Watch, the
Legal Aid Foundation and the Pemuda Hindu Bali demanded an
investigation and lodged a complaint with the Administrative Court
in Denpasar was not mentioned by the *Bali Post*. The court rejected
the allegation.

When Dewa Made Beratha was inaugurated on 28 August 2003, the building used by the provincial assembly was heavily protected by police, army and PDI-P militia. No incidents occurred. The re-election of the governor was decided in favour of "Jakarta" and marked the defeat of regional autonomy, but it came at a price. According to a detailed reconstruction by the magazine *Sarad*, 38 PDI-P members of the provincial assembly had received in total Rp 5.5 billion (US$550,000) from their party.[10] Bali's police chief Mangku Pastika stated, however, that no bribery had occurred because the case had not caused a loss to the state. Moreover, he added: "There is no term for 'money politics' in our laws."[11]

2004: National Elections and the "Absence of Cimax"

Despite rising tensions between PDI-P and Golkar and violent incidents in October 2003, the campaigns for the elections of the national parliament and the provincial and district assemblies of 5 April 2004 were not disturbed by big incidents, but neither were they characterised by great enthusiasm. Compared to the passion of 1999, the elections of 2004 were a routine affair.

Ajeg would remain the key word used to domesticate the ambitions of national parties and to pacify the campaign. During its 40th anniversary in October 2003, Golkar launched the slogan "*Ajeg* Bali is Golkar's desire."[12] In February 2004 political parties agreed to guarantee peace and order while the military promised to keep an eye on the campaigns as well. And indeed, few incidents occurred.[13]

The village of Blahkiuh felt little tension despite the uneasy relationship between the controversial brothers, who were both prominent leaders in the PDI-P, and their own neighbourhood. The main topic of discussion and *warung* (coffee shop/foodstall) gossip was that several people had left PDI-P and established branches of small parties, such as Partai Indonesia Baru and Partai Pelopor.[14] But apart from the activities of local candidates seeking election to the regional or provincial council, nothing much happened. On Election Day the mayor of Denpasar urged people to wear *adat* dress in order to give expression to *Ajeg*

Bali. Villagers in Blahkiuh saw the irony of urban voters dressed in *adat* costume, saying, "We don't need that, because we still know what *adat* is about."

The election results showed that the Mega-hysteria of 1999 was over. Under Megawati's presidency school fees and other costs of living had risen, and corruption had become a very visible phenomenon in provincial and district politics. Now PDI-P's share of the vote went down from 79.5 per cent to 51.7 per cent and Golkar climbed from 10.5 per cent to 17.5 per cent, while new parties like Partai Demokrat (5.5 per cent) and Tutut's PKPB (4.2 per cent) captured smaller shares of the votes. The remaining votes went to a number of small parties, some of them Islamic. In terms of seats PDI-P still managed to maintain its majority, while Golkar made a modest comeback:

Elections April 2004[15]

DPRD Bali	Total Number of Seats	PDI-P	Golkar
1999	340	261	37
2004	355	202	77

Interestingly PDI-P lost a lot of votes in Badung (from 77.7 per cent to 47.2 per cent), probably because many people resented the outcome of the gubernatorial elections. In Gianyar Golkar, with the support of *puri* Ubud, experienced a remarkable revival (from 7.4 per cent to 32.5 per cent).[16] In Blahkiuh the two PDI-P brothers were defeated in their own hamlet by Golkar but still won a majority in the village as a whole.

In Denpasar the connection between *preman* and party politics resurfaced briefly when Wayan D., chairman of the Denpasar market association and PDI-P cadre responsible for the ranking order of the PDI-P candidates for the election, was physically attacked by a couple of strongmen.

Initially it looked as if the incident had to do with a controversy over a payment of market tax, but Wayan D. revealed that he had been threatened by the leader of the FPD, Made Minggik. It turned out that a son of Minggik, who was a PDI-P candidate, was not elected. Wayan D. was blamed for having put him low on the list of party candidates, effectively ensuring that his candidacy would fail. The case attracted extensive newspaper coverage, but showed also how reluctant the editors were to expose Minggik's involvement. When Wayan D. finally came back from his hiding place he went to Minggik's house in order to offer his apologies for his "unfounded allegations" about being threatened. Eventually Minggik showed his benevolence and agreed to a reconciliation.[17]

Minggik's power depended to a large extent on the alliance between his Forum Peduli Denpasar and mayor Puspayoga, *puri* Satria and the PDI-P. Since both *puri* Satria and the PDI-P had lost at least some of their influence, chief of police Mangku Pastika saw now a possibility to reduce the power of Minggik and his men. He "invaded" Minggik's core domain, the Ubung bus terminal where he disarmed his private security force. Minggik was furious and demanded apologies, but Mangku Pastika ordered mayor Puspayoga to come to the police headquarters where he had to make a public statement in support of the police chief.[18] A final showdown between Mangku Pastika and Minggik did not occur, but Minggik knew that he had to keep a low profile, at least for the time being.

It is no coincidence that Mangku Pastika simultaneously launched an island-wide campaign against illegal cock fights, which were controlled in many places by gangs that had close connections with PDI-P.

Clifford Geertz once wrote that Balinese social life was characterised by an absence of climax.[19] The grounds on which he made this statement are questionable, but it cannot be denied that political developments in Bali after October 1999 lacked climax. The *Ajeg* Bali campaign was in this respect instrumental because it silenced controversies and neutralised debates between political opponents.

After the elections of April 2004 few people were excited by the idea that there were still two more rounds of the presidential elections to come. Seen from a national perspective and counting in terms of absolute numbers, Bali was not very important for the main contenders for the presidency and Megawati showed little interest in her constituency in Bali. She did not show up at the

Illustration 6: PDI-P flag with Megawati's portrait in Blahkiuh (photo by the author)

Illustration 7: Minggik giving a public statement (*Radar Bali*, 17 Apr. 2004)

opening of the Bali Art Festival, although the event was specially rescheduled to fit her agenda. "She forgot us, so why should we remember her?" was an often-heard conclusion. Megawati also lost the support of the re-elected governor Dewa Made Beratha. Like his colleague Sutiyoso in Jakarta, he wisely remained neutral despite Megawati's active role in his re-election one year before.

Meanwhile Susilo Bambang Yudhoyono (SBY for short) and his running mate, Yusuf Kalla, also adopted the concept of *"Ajeg Bali"* in their campaign slogans. In Badung Megawati's campaign team emphasised her civilian background in contrast with the military background of her main rivals. Therefore they launched a slogan with the term *"civil society"* in it, which was for most villagers totally incomprehensible and even unpronounceable. In Gianyar Megawati's campaign demonstrated more common sense, emphasising her Balinese origins and her ambition to sustain *Ajeg Bali*.

It did not help much. In July Megawati won 54.9 per cent of the votes in Bali, while SBY won 31.8 per cent and Wiranto 10.4. In the final round in September Megawati was defeated by SBY, although she still had managed to get 62.3 per cent of the votes in Bali, while SBY obtained 37.7 per cent. In contrast to the riots in October 1999, no anger erupted this time when it became clear that Mega was defeated.

Although electoral democracy functioned quite well in Bali, people became fatigued by the many elections held within such a short period of time. Moreover, many people were disappointed by the absence of institutional democracy, as district assemblies turned out to be hotbeds of corruption where personal and party interests prevailed.

2005: Regional Elections[20]

The regional elections of 2005 took place within the framework of a new law, no. 32/2004, which replaced law no. 22/1999 on regional administration. The main difference between the two laws concerned the position of the district head and the provincial governor. They were no longer elected by the assembly of the district or the province, but directly chosen by the people. Moreover, the new heads of districts and provinces were no longer primarily accountable to district or provincial assemblies but instead reported directly to the Minister of the Interior. This meant a considerable decline in the bargaining power of the district and provincial assemblies because they lost their grip on the head of the administration. On their part the newly elected administrators would depend more than before, on the central government, but they would have more room to manoeuvre within their district or province, where their authority was from now on based on a popular mandate.[21]

In June 2005 for the first time in history direct elections for 11 governors, 176 district heads and 36 mayors were held in Indonesia. In Bali, four district heads and one mayor were elected on June 24. Marcus Mietzner has observed that throughout Indonesia political parties played a less dominant role during the regional elections, while he also pointed at the successful rise of independent candidates.[22] A similar process took place in Bali. Compared to previous elections political parties and especially the PDI-P played a less prominent role, giving way to the emergence of independent candidates, with whom Golkar made strategic alliances.

Friendly Visits

To rule out any possibility of violent confrontations, the authorities in Bali mobilised a security force of 16,000 men from the police, the army and local civilian groups. Furthermore, candidates agreed not to campaign in tourists areas in order to preserve the continuity of tourism.

Compared to previous campaigns that featured pop stars with so-called *dangdut* performances and masses of young man who received t-shirts and money to attend rallies, a new phenomenon occurred. Apart from a few mass gatherings, candidates paid numerous visits to temples, *banjar*, and irrigation associations (*subak*) where they asked the people for their support. These visits were called *medharma suaka*, a Balinese response to the Islamic word *silaturahmi*, or friendly visit. The term also referred to the visit of a bridegroom to the house of his future parents in law to ask permission to marry their daughter. Phrased in this way, candidates were male leaders courting a female constituency. Some critics called this procedure "primordial" because it favoured collective voting behaviour.[23] Others saw it as an example of the way modern democracy was localised in a Balinese environment.

In many cases *banjar* or temple congregations held lengthy discussions in order to decide which candidate they would support, after which they would invite their favourite to come have a visit. During these visits the candidate was expected to give a contribution of Rp. one to three million (US$100–300) to the temple, or he promised a larger sum of money if he was indeed elected. Candidates refrained from giving large sums of money in advance, having seen how during the elections in April 2004 PDI-P had spent a fortune without getting the votes party leaders had hoped for. The magazine *Sarad* estimated that on average candidates had to raise Rp. five billion (US$500,000) to finance their campaigns, and that in total Rp. 65 billion was spent by 13 candidates.[24] There was already one winner even before the elections were held: Satria Naradha. In his capacity as chairman of the *Kooperasi Krama Bali* he received substantial donations from all the candidates who wanted favourable publicity by the Bali Post Group.

Below I will briefly review the campaigns in the various districts. In general, the outcomes of the elections were mixed. In three districts PDI-P candidates managed to stay in power, whereas in two other districts new independent candidates, who had allied themselves with Golkar, gained a victory.

Consolidation

In terms of caste relations the district elections did not offer a final showdown between aristocracy and commoners. Neither the aristocratic "*puri*" managed to make an overall come back, nor did commoners succeed in finally depriving the nobility of its power. The administrative positions at stake were eventually filled by three commoners and two members of the nobility.

In Bangli, Denpasar and Tabanan the incumbent PDI-P administrators were all re-elected. In Bangli I Nengah Arnawa won easily 70 per cent of the votes. He used his position as district head to distribute large government subsidies. Each village in Bangli received Rp. 50 million (US$5,000), rendering it virtually impossible for the other candidates to raise any criticism. During a public debate between the candidates the moderator was so anxious to avoid disagreement or any reference to sensitive issues that angry supporters of one of the other candidates almost started a fight.

Ironically candidates of noble descent won the elections in the biggest town in Bali. Mayor Anak Agung Puspayoga from *puri* Satria, and his running mate Ida Bagus Rai Mantra, son of a popular governor of Bali and successful entrepreneur, won an easy victory in Denpasar, with 70 per cent of the votes. A.A. Puspayoga had a decent track record in the sense that he had kept his promises regarding the improvement of local infrastructure. Moreover, as a prominent member of *puri* Satria he showed his generosity by promising poor families the opportunity to participate in a grand post-cremation ritual, the so-called *maligia jangkep* which was held on 4 August 2005 in order to commemorate the victims of the *Puputan Badung* in 1906, during which the souls of the deceased are released from their attachments to the material world.[25] A reasonable administrative performance and royal generosity proved a powerful combination. Furthermore he could still rely on the loyal support of the strongmen from Forum Peduli Denpasar (FPD).[26]

Puspayoga also benefited from internal weaknesses in the alliance between Golkar, *puri* Pamecutan and Laskar Bali. After the leader of *puri* Pamecutan was convicted of killing his half-brother, the former royal family was split. A descendant of *puri* Peguyangan emerged as the Golkar candidate, while his running mate — the older brother of the leader of the Laskar Bali — came from *puri* Tegal. With the support of Laskar Bali the Golkar candidates presented themselves as aristocrats who maintained close ties with the people. But despite their slogan "born in the *puri*, raised among the people", and their efforts to mobilise support among the large migrant communities in Denpasar, they failed to defeat the strong alliance between PDI-P, *puri* Satria and the FPD. A significant number of people (40 per cent), presumably including a large segment of the migrant population in Denpasar, did not vote.

In Tabanan the incumbent district head I Nyoman Adi Wiryatama and his ruling PDI-P did not encounter many problems either. With a running mate from a branch of the old royal family, Wiryatama did not face a serious challenge and won 66 per cent of the votes. Despite this comfortable majority and the dominant position of PDI-P in Tabanan, various instances of violence and intimidation were reported. It is public knowledge that Wiryatama maintains cordial relationships with various groups of *preman* in Tabanan — to the extent that he is called *bupati preman* — and this connection helps to explain the relatively violent nature of his campaign. In return for their support many groups of *preman* who are deeply involved in illegal gambling, demanded from the district head a formal decision to legalise cock fights being an integral part of Balinese culture. This brought the district head into direct confrontation with chief of police Mangku Pastika, who had launched an island-wide campaign against gambling and cock fights.

The Emergence of Independent Leaders

Thus in Bangli, Denpasar and Tabanan, PDIP-P managed to maintain the power positions it had conquered in 1999. The situation in Karangesem was to some extent similar to that in Tabanan. In 1999 a new PDI-P administrator, I Gede Sumantara, was in charge, supported by a group of *preman* led by Kari Subali. However, despite the fact that Megawati came personally to Karangasem to support his candidacy, I Gede Sumantara lost the election. Sumantara's term as administrator had been controversial. He was known as a very authoritarian administrator — even to the point of beating up one of his lower officials — but he had failed to turn the local PDI-P into a strong party machine. He received only 30 per cent of the votes cast.

Other contenders for the district leadership included a descendent of the royal family of Karangasem. This man was the grandson of the last king of Karangasem and the son of a former district head, but he failed to gain a significant share of the votes. Because he had lived for a long period in Jakarta, he was not well-known, and people were not inclined to support a rather anonymous candidate simply because he was a descendant of the old royal family.

The winner of the election in Karangasem was an independent outsider, I Wayan Geredeg, who had allied himself loosely with Golkar by choosing the chairman of the local party branch as his running mate. I Wayan Geredeg was a successful self-made man who had become a wealthy entrepreneur. Born to a poor family, he migrated to Denpasar after the devastating eruption of Mount Agung in 1963 and he worked his way from daily wage laborer to well-connected contractor. As such he became both patron and role model for the thousands of migrants from Karangasem in Denpasar who supported his candidacy with great enthusiasm. A telling example of his entrepreneurial attitude was a campaign to repair damaged roads in Karangasem which he organised and paid personally. The combination of personal charisma, private capital, the political experience of Golkar, and the informal support of a leading *preman* won I Wayan Geredeg 37 per cent of the votes in a hotly contested election involving four candidates.[27]

Badung: The Return of *puri* Mengwi

Whereas a few years earlier outsiders had tried to gain control of local PDI-P branches in Jembrana and Buleleng in order to seize power at the district level, during the 2005 elections in Karangasem and Badung the PDI-P was defeated by new independent leaders who challenged its hegemony.

The campaign that received most media coverage occurred in Badung, where PDI-P had experienced an internal crisis that weakened the party considerably. The incumbent district head Cokorda Ratmadi (2000–5) from *puri* Satria was not allowed to stand for re-election. Apparently PDI-P headquarters in Jakarta vetoed his candidacy because he had resisted party policy during the gubernatorial elections in 2003. In his place the vice-district head, I Made Sumer became the PDI-P candidate in Badung. Made Sumer came from Kuta where he had an interest in the tourist industry, and was supported by other entrepreneurs in the tourist sector who financed his campaign. He was supported by the textile tycoon Putu Agus Antara, who was also the main sponsor of the Garuda Wisnu Kencana project. However, towards the end of the campaign Made Sumer ran out of money. Rumours indicated that Made Sumer's campaign team had embezzled large sums.

Made Sumer was challenged by Anak Agung Gde Agung from the old royal house of Mengwi, who presented himself as an independent candidate representing the interests of ordinary peasants in the northern part of the district. Whereas Megawati Sukarnoputri tended to support candidates who turned out to be very unpopular, Golkar was eager to support candidates who could rely on a strong constituency. In doing so Golkar tried to make a come back at the district level in Bali. Gde Agung's running mate was I Nyoman Sukerta from Kuta, chairman of Golkar in Badung who had made a fortune in the tourist business. Reportedly he earned large profits (with Tommy Suharto) from land transactions in Pecatu on the southern peninsula.

Since PDI-P candidate Made Sumer himself came from Kuta in the south, he chose a man from the lower nobility from Mengwi, in the north, as his running mate. This person was the rather anonymous son of a famous and respected irrigation head in Mengwi in the 1970s. To some extent the contest between Made Sumer from Kuta and Gde Agung from Mengwi became a confrontation between the urbanised tourist area of south Badung and the rural areas of northern Badung. Northern Badung coincides more or less with the old kingdom of Mengwi and during the campaign Gde Agung presented himself as a descendant of the old dynasty and a son of Mengwi, which had been conquered by the kingdom of Badung in 1891 and for too long neglected by southern administrators.[28] In terms of absolute numbers Gde Agung seemingly had an advantage as the northern part had 142,000 inhabitants whereas the south — without the city of Denpasar, which forms a separate *kotamadya* — counted 135,000 people. However, many people in northern places like Petang, Carangsari, Penarungan and Sedang, were for historical reasons anti-*puri* Mengwi and supported Made Sumer.

Gde Agung emphasised the need to improve agriculture, education and health care and deliberately identified with his constituency

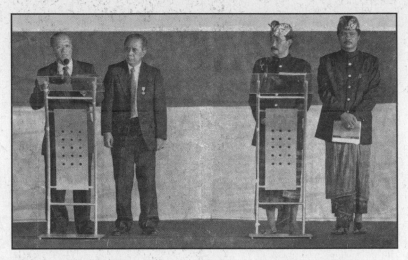

Illustration 8: Debate between candidates in Badung. Left Made Sumer and running mate; right Gede Agung and his running mate. Note the differences in dress and posture.
(*Bali Post*, 9 June 2005)

by dressing in *adat* clothes. Many informants said that they liked this look, which made him appear smart and added to his authority. Compared to the suits worn by his opponents, which represented a corrupt and inefficient type of politician, *adat* dress made a far better impression and radiated charisma. People said Gede Agung's moustache added to his appeal as well.

Against the dichotomies between the neglected northern and the prosperous southern parts of Badung, and between good *adat* and bad politics, which were emphasised by Gde Agung, Made Sumer presented a distinction between nobility — and especially the revival of "feudal" rule embodied by *puri* Mengwi — and the interests of the ordinary people represented by Made Sumer and his PDI-P. Large banners supporting Made Sumer represented the elections as a choice between "feudalism" and "democracy", and he was in this respect openly supported by the large Pasek organisation.

Gde Agung countered this accusation in an ambiguous way. He clearly embodied the political revival of *puri* Mengwi, and relied on the old charisma of the dynasty in matters concerning irrigation and fertility, and used the front yard of the old dynastic temple *Pura* Taman Ayun as the headquarters of his campaign. He was also fortunate to receive covert support from *puri* Satria — once the arch-enemy of Mengwi but motivated by internal troubles in the PDI-P to become an ally for the time being.

The alliance between *puri* Mengwi and *puri* Satria reinforced the impression that the election was basically a choice between aristocracy and commoners. This perception was reinforced by Anak Agung Kusuma Wardana — who had played a leading role on the Padanggalak case — when he stated that Bali will only remain *ajeg*, or firm, as long as it is ruled by descendents of the old royal dynasties. However, Gde Agung managed to neutralise this "feudal" image. On the one hand he emphasised the importance of agriculture and promised to improve irrigation facilities, on the other hand he pointed at the crucial role of the old royal temples in the mountains, the centre and at the coast which had to secure the continuity of fertility. It followed then that he — representing both the old dynasty and the government — would be the ideal candidate to foster prosperity.

Apart from the north-south divide, and the distinctions between *adat* and politics, and between nobility and commoners, another issue proved eventually to be more decisive. Long before the official campaign began, Gde Agung had manifested himself as an honest, hard working man, who had set himself the task of serving the interests of the people, and in this connection he had visited numerous irrigation and temple associations. This type of *medharma suaka*, or friendly visit, was also appreciated as *merakyat*, socialising with the people. People appreciated the fact that he had visited them over the preceding months, and not just during the formal campaign, to listen to their wishes. "I did not vote for him because he has royal blood," someone in Blahkiuh told me, "it was because of these visits that I gave him the benefit of the doubt."

Like any other campaign in Indonesia this one was also concluded with a large gathering for which thousands of people were mobilised. Creating traffic jams, "*bikin macet*", is an important means of visualising a person's power, especially in the final phase of a political campaign. After Gde Agung attended a mass gathering in Blahkiuh where 10,000 people had shown up, the final confrontation with Made Sumer took place. Made Sumer staged a provocative mass meeting in the vicinity of Mengwi that was attended by Megawati, who addressed a crowd of 15,000 people. Two days later Gde Agung held his climactic final meeting in Mengwi where he mobilised no less that 35,000 people. People knew already by then that Made Sumer was defeated.

On 24 June Gde Agung did indeed win the elections by gaining 55 per cent of the votes. In Blahkiuh, the two brothers who belonged to the establishment of the PDI-P faced another humiliating setback. Their candidate, Made Sumer, was not only defeated in their *banjar*, but even within their own neighbourhood.

The elections of district heads in Karangasem and Badung not only show that electoral democracy has taken root in Bali, but also that a healthy countervailing power has emerged that challenges the dominance of political parties at the local level. What remains to be seen is the extent to which the newly elected leaders are willing and able to make local government more democratic.

CHAPTER 8

Beyond *Ajeg* Bali

O n October 12 2005 I Gede Winasa was re-elected as district head of Jembrana. The hegemonic position he has managed to achieve was illustrated by the fact that he won no less that 89 per cent of the votes.[1] Perhaps even more amazing was that a few months earlier, his wife, Ratna Ani Lestari, had been elected as district head of Banyuwangi in neighboring East Java. This made them the first married couple to run two adjacent districts. Despite the appearance of hegemony, people soon started to cast doubt about the religious reliability of both Winasa and his wife. In order to be elected in Banyuwangi, Ratna Ani Lestari had changed her religion: she was no longer a Hindu and presented herself as a pious Muslim. However, Muslim leaders in Banyuwangi did not trust her and started a campaign to prevent her inauguration as district head.[2] At the same time people in Bali wondered whether I Gede Winasa was actually a reliable Hindu. If both Winasa and his wife were unreliable opportunists, how could the entrance gate of Bali, where thousands of Javanese Muslim migrants entered the island, be properly controlled?

Anti-Muslim sentiments erupted once more in March 2006, when the national parliament in Jakarta discussed a new anti-pornography law (*UU Anti Porngrafi dan Pornoaksi*). The draft law also stipulated that one was not allowed to show "sensual parts of the body" in public, and forbade erotic dances and kissing in public. Especially these clauses caused a furious Bali wide protest.

The law was seen as an explicit attempt by Muslims to cripple Balinese culture and the tourist industry. Balinese civil society showed its strength by organising a broad alliance against the law — consisting of public intellectuals, artists, *adat* institutions, the tourist sector and the *Bali Post* — which compelled the governor and the provincial parliament to make public statements in which they rejected the law. The protest was fuelled by a so-called *somasi* (legal grievance) by the Majelis Mujahidin Indonesia, which accused the governor of Bali of arrogance and separatism, and stated that tourism had enslaved the Balinese by bringing all sorts of vices to the island. When a delegation of the national parliament visited the governor of Bali on 12 March to discuss the matter, a provocative cultural manifestation attended by a large crowd was held in front of his office.[3] The manifestation included sensual dances like *joged*, fashion and drag queen shows, and performances by punk and reggae bands. The law was temporarily postponed.

In September 2006, on the occasion of the commemoration marking 100 years since the *puputan* Badung, Islam featured as an important subtext. This time the usual commemoration of the *puputan* by descendents of the old dynasty and government officials was somewhat sidelined by a brand new purification ritual, the so-called Grebeg Aksara Prasada. Initiated by public intellectuals and consisting of processions, cleansing rituals and performances, the event aimed to achieve spiritual renewal by reviving the values of the golden era of the realm of Majapahit (thirteenth–fifteenth century). According to Balinese chronicles the conquest of Bali by the Javanese kingdom of Majapahit in 1343 had brought civilisation to the island. The ritual in September 2006 aimed to commemorate and revitalise the Buddhist, Shivaite and royal aspects of Majapahit. When I interviewed one of the organisers and asked her how we should situate Islam in all this, she said: "Islam is exactly what worries me most."[4] These cases once again illustrate in different ways the anti-immigrant *cum* anti-Muslim attitude that is one of the driving forces of the *Ajeg* Bali movement.

In Bali regional autonomy and electoral democracy did not automatically result in better governance. Instead, both processes reinforced the entrenchment of Balinese identity politics

Illustration 9: "How to get out?"
(*Sarad* 43, 2003)

represented by urban middle-class intellectuals. *Ajeg* Bali erases a discourse about citizenship that forms the very basis of democracy. Moreover, decentralisation in Bali has produced an administrative fragmentation that threatens to undermine regional autonomy. It is ironic that despite all efforts to achieve purification and moral renewal, corruption is widespread in administrative circles.[5]

It is a paradox that Balinese middle-class intellectuals tend to stress their regional authenticity (and deny their Indonesian identity) in a very *Indonesian* way. Throughout the archipelago differences are increasingly expressed in similar terms, as seminars held in various parts of the country to explore the particular nature of local identities adopt a uniform and distinctly Indonesian format.[6] Therefore one may question the special Balinese character of the *Ajeg* Bali campaign, and wonder to what extent it is part of a larger *Indonesian* phenomenon.

It is not only in terms of identity politics that Bali remains part of Indonesia. The island has also experienced the rise of political parties and *preman*, and the first manifestations of electoral democracy. Decentralisation and the regional articulation of *reformasi* have resulted in the rise of new political figures who are based in a dynamic urban middle-class. Kings and Brahmans no longer authorise Balinese culture. Instead, people like Satria Naradha provide public definitions of "the essence" of Bali. But despite hegemonic efforts to formulate a reassuring self image that keeps Muslims at a distance and invites tourists to visit Bali, Balinese intellectuals face an enormous challenge: how can Bali survive in a wider global context?

The dilemma of Bali as an open fortress cannot be resolved because an open economy and a closed cultural identity are not compatible. In contrast to the dominant view that defines Balinese culture as essentially Hindu and anchored in village *adat*, Degung Santikarma (2001b) has written:

> Living in the midst of the trans-national traffic jam that is Bali can be an exhausting experience. For gloBALIsation has not just shipped bamboo wind chimes and leering wooden cats out to the boutiques of Berkeley and Brisbane, or seen Bill Clinton and Bay Watch battling for television airtime in the *banjar*, but has opened new markets for that most precious commodity of the new cultural capitalism: authenticity.

Balinese are eager to export newly invented cultural authenticities, and the new middle class leadership seems to be very capable in defining the basic ingredients and core values of Balinese culture. The problem, however, with essentialist concepts that express hegemonic ambitions such as *Ajeg* Bali is that they are based on post-colonial models that refer to closed and homogeneous societies, and cannot incorporate notions of change and agency. The late professor Ngurah Bagus, who was very concerned about Bali's future, urged Balinese intellectuals on several occasions to face the world with critical open-mindedness instead of relying on a static and inward looking attitude.[7]

One of the biggest challenges facing Balinese administrators and intellectuals is to develop a more dynamic idea of their culture that offers room for hybridity and transnational dimensions. For how long and to what extent can a concerned urban middle-class that maintains an emphasis on authenticity and a rigid defence of an exclusive ethnic profile of Bali co-exist with the ongoing formation of a new transnational urban corridor stretching from Bangkok, through Kuala Lumpur, Singapore, Jakarta, and Surabaya to Bali?[8] As the new cleansing ritual in September 2006 demonstrates, Bali harbours a vibrant cultural vitality and creativity. Moreover, customary village institutions and urban middle-class initiatives demonstrate the resilience of civil society in Bali. It is therefore challenging to imagine how an open-minded, self-confident, well-regulated and outward looking Bali, as a cultural counterpart of a business metropolis like Singapore might appear in the future.

Notes

Chapter 1

1. See also Satria Naradha 2004.
2. There is a vast literature on this topic; see for overviews amongst others Aspinall and Fealy 2003; Erb *et al.* 2005; and Schulte Nordholt and Van Klinken 2007. Where relevant I will refer to the wider national context in the following chapters.
3. Picard 1999: 16; see also Bateson 1970; Schulte Nordholt 1999.
4. Picard 1996, 2003. Picard refers in this respect to the term *Kebalian*, or Balineseness.
5. Burhan Magenda 1989: 387. In December 1946 Bali and Flores had become part of the Negara Indonesia Timur. From 1950–54 Bali belonged to the province Sunda Ketjil that was renamed in 1954 as Nusa Tenggara.
6. See Robinson 1995.
7. See for instance Smith-Kipp (1992) on North Sumatra and Pemberton (1994) on Java.

Chapter 2

1. Data in this section are derived from *Bali Membangun* 2003; *Bali Post* 16 Aug. 2003; *Jakarta Post,* 25 May 2003; *Kompas* 12 Mar. 2001, MacRae 1997; Picard 1996, 2003, 2005; Pringle 2004; Putu Suasta 2001.
2. Picard 1996; Pringle 2004.
3. Although many people in Bali complain that tourism underwent a serious crisis after 2001, the figures suggest only a slight decline. It is possible that package tours continued to bring large numbers of tourists (from Taiwan, Korea, and Russia) to the island, but that these groups are concentrated in a few places and spend less money.

4. In 1990 26 per cent of the population lived in urban areas. Both in (former) rural as well as well as in urban areas there has been a rapid commoditisation of land, even to the extent that in urban areas poorer people are no longer able to pay their land tax, which is based on the estimated market price, and are being forced to sell their land and move to cheaper places.

5. Aditjondro 1995. Ida Bagus Oka (1988–98) was a medical professor and had been rector of Udayana University. His predecessor Ida Bagus Mantra (1978–88) had also an academic background. Contrary to his successor, Mantra was actively involved in discussions about religious and cultural matters.

6. *Far Eastern Economic Review* [hereafter FEER], 26 May 1994; Warren 1994; Putu Suasta and Connor 1999.

7. An instrumental role was played by I Made Samba, head of the district planning board (Bappeda) of Tabanan, who was also head of the Tabanan branch of Parisada Hindu Dharma.

8. At about the same time a successful Islamic protest was organised in Jakarta against a lottery in which the presidential family was involved. This proved that religion would be a good strategy to voice protest. Nyoman Darma Putra, personal communication.

9. For a listing of the involvement of the presidential family in tourist projects, see a report by George Aditjondro, *Apakabar* 5 June 1997. The list includes the PT Pecatu Graha housing project of Tommy Suharto in the vicinity of Nusa Dua. Landowners there received compensation of only Rp. 2.5 million per *are*, although the prevailing market price was 20–30 million per *are*. The project never materialised and the dispute between former landowners and PT Pecatu Graha remains unresolved.

10. *FEER,* 26 May 1994.

11. Schulte Nordholt 2001: 66–8.

12. Support was given by the well-known regional historian Ketut Subandi who argued that the beach was a sacred place because in ancient times the ancestor of the Balinese Brahmans (including Governor Ida Bagus Oka) had rested there during one of his journeys. Megawati Sukarnoputri, who had become a political martyr since she was in 1996 ousted as leader of the PDI by the government, supported the protest as well.

13. See photo on the cover.

14. *Jakarta Post,* 14 Aug. 2000, 14 Mar. 2002; *Newsweek,* 1 Feb. 1999; *FEER,* 31 Oct. 2002.

15. *Jakarta Post,* 14 Aug. 2001.

16. See Moor (2003) for a detailed account of the attack and the arrest of the perpetrators.

17. Bakker 2003. My assistant who earned his money as a motor taxi (*ojek*) driver had to pay in 2004 Rp. 4.4 million for school fees for his three children.
18. Organised by *desa adat* Kuta, the regional government of Badung, and the provincial government of Bali, the ceremony was conducted by five priests, and involved the sacrifice of 79 animals.
19. Tourist arrivals dropped by 22 per cent in November 2005, *Jakarta Post*, 3 Jan. 2006.
20. Cf. Robinson 1995: 9–14.
21. *Bali Arts and Culture Newsletter*, 1 Mar. 2001. One of the artists criticised was Nyoman Nuarta, designer of the Garuda Wisnu Kencana statue.
22. *Jakarta Post*, 13 Jan. 2001 and 8 Apr. 2002. *Apakabar/Clarknet*, 23 Aug. 1998.
23. The demonstration temporarily cooled down growing tensions between Golkar and PDI-P. Couteau 2002: 24; *International Crisis Group* [hereafter ICG] 2003: 5; *Jakarta Post* 30 Jan. 2002; Vickers 2002.
24. *Apakabar/Clarknet*, 13 Feb. 1997, 24 May 1997; *Bali Post* 25 Mar. 1997.
25. E-mail Rucina Ballinger, 10 Oct. 1998.
26. *Bali Post*, 21 Oct. 1999, 23 Oct. 1999; Couteau 2002: 243–5.
27. Ketut Ardhana (2004) has pointed at the continuation of aristocratic rule at the regional level in Bali. But the examples he mentions, *puri* Gianyar and *puri* Satria in Denpasar, turned out to be exceptions, because in 2005 the majority of the new rulers in Bali were commoners. See for the elections of 2005, Chapter 7.
28. *Bali Post*, Aug., Sept., Nov. 2003; *Jawa Pos*, 24 Nov. 2003

Chapter 3

1. Schulte Nordholt 1999.
2. Picard 1999; Ramstedt 2002, 2004. Ramstedt (2002: 149–50) notes an interesting difference between Balinese and orientalist discourses regarding Bali, because European orientalists emphasised the egalitarian qualities of *adat* and the hierarchical nature of Hinduism.
3. Schulte Nordholt 1999.
4. See Bakker 1993.
5. Howe 2001: 148.
6. In 1997 there were reportedly seven million Hindus in Indonesia, which implies that there were more Hindus outside Bali than on the island. Many of these new Hindus were people who had not (yet) an officially recognised religion (*belum beragama*) and had found shelter in Hinduism.

7. See Subandi 1982. Especially some Pasek subgroups like the Pasek Gelgel increased considerably in numbers as they accepted many new families whose ancestry was not clear.
8. Pitana 1999, 2001.
9. Ramstedt 2002: 160–1.
10. Ngurah Bagus 2004.
11. Concerned that Balinese are about losing their language recently *Bali Post* started to publish a Balinese language lift-out.
12. Cf. Howe 2001. After the ending of the Cold War contacts between Bali and India were resumed. While in India a reorientation towards the Pacific occurred, a new flow of affluent pilgrims travelled from Bali to India, resulting in a new wave of Indianisation in Bali (Ramstedt 2004: 17–21). Although groups in the ruling political party in India, BJP, favoured the active support of the Hindu diaspora abroad, Prime Minister Atal Bihari Vajpayee refused to support Hindus in Bali officially. When Governor Made Beratha met the Indian prime minister during his visit to India in October 2003 he stated that many of the Hindus of his island had lost touch with the Hindus of India and that, as a result, their religious and cultural practices were losing their meaning (*Asia Times,* 22 Oct. 2003).
13. Cf. Howe 2001: 76, 83, 133.
14. Ibid.
15. Peraturan Menteri Dalam Negeri no. 11/1984; Perda no. 6/1986 and no. 12/1988.
16. See above; cf. Warren 2000.
17. In the south Balinese village where I have lived, each *banjar* was represented by two persons who were chosen by the *banjar* council.
18. Warren 2004; *Sarad* 36, 2003. *Adat* is originally an Arab word. Unlike the situation in West Sumatra where the *nagari* has replaced the New Order village, in Bali the *desa dinas* has not disappeared and still provides basic services such as the issuing of identity cards and so on.
19. *Bali Post,* 20 Mar. 2002; Warren 2004.
20. *Radar Bali,* 7 June 2001. In 2003 and 2004 villages received Rp. 20 and Rp. 25 million from the provincial government (*Bali Post,* 25 Mar. 2004).
21. Warren 2004. Between 2002 and 2004 the number of *desa pakraman* increased from 1366 to 1417. It is not clear whether this increase, or *pemekaran,* was motivated by a desire for more government subsidies (personal communication Ketut Sumarta, June 2004).
22. A negative aspect of increased ritual activities is the pressure by village elites on ordinary villagers to contribute large amounts of money for temple restoration and the accompanying rituals. In Ubud, for instance, it is not unusual that people who earn a modest amount of

Rp. 20.000 per day are requested to pay, on top of their normal ritual obligations, Rp. 250.000 for these purposes (*Sarad* 39, 2003).
23. *Sarad* 39, 2003; Bali Post, 27 May 2004.
24. Parimartha 2003.

Chapter 4

1. *Sarad* 31, 2002; *Suara Merdeka* 10 July 1997; *ICG* 2003.
2. Widnyani and Widia 2002.
3. In the old days *pecalang* did not belong to the village sphere. In nineteenth century Mengwi they were agents/spies acting on behalf of the royal centre (Schulte Nordholt 1996: 150). In Java they were policemen, spies (Pigeaud 1938).
4. In 2002, 875 krisses from the *pecalang* of Denpasar were consecrated in the sacred temple Pura Dalem Ped, on the island of Nusa Penida, which is dedicated to the god Ratu Gede Macaling. The ritual was sponsored by the surf company Quicksilver in Benoa.
5. Santikarma 2001a.
6. Santikarma (2002) talks in this context of a militarisation of culture. Ironically, in 1999 *pecalang* in Kuta managed to marginalise the role of the military, who used to collect protection money from street vendors (*ICG* 2003).
7. In the Nusa Dua area, where many five star hotels are located, a small group of 36 *pecalang* received each Rp. 500.000 per month, while they also had a minivan and a computer at their disposal. In Tabanan and in Seminyak *pecalang* were involved in illegal gambling and prostitution (*Sarad* 31, 2002; *Bali Post*, 12 Aug. 2003; *Tempo*, 16 Oct. 2003).
8. *Sarad* 44, 2003.
9. Based on reports in *Bali Post*, 21/25 July 2003.
10. *Sarad* 49, 2004.
11. *Bali Post*, 25/26 Feb. 2004, 4 Mar. 2004; *Jawa Pos*, 27 Feb. 2004.
12. Based on reports in *Jakarta Post*, 5 June 2002; *Sarad* 7, 2000; 44, 2003. This time Wayan Sudirta defended the 45 families who were expelled from the village. Other cases include a conflict on the sale of one ha. of village land to a businessman in Abiantuwung in Jan. 2002. The houses of 30 families who had objected to the sale were burnt (*Jakarta Post*, 10 Jan. 2002). In Feb. 2002 the houses of seven Christian families in Kintamani were burnt because they allegedly had ignored their obligations towards the village (*Jakarta Post*, 16 Feb. 2002).
13. Based on reports in *Bali Post* 9/17 Sept. 2003.
14. *Bali Post*, 22 Aug. 2003. The disputed land had been *sawah pecatu*, which was given to followers (*pengayah*) from *puri* Ubud in exchange for loyalty and services, after Ubud's victory in local warfare at the end of the nineteenth century.

15. *Bali Post,* 24 Apr. 2004; *Radar Bali,* 13 Apr. 2004. The word "feudal" was used because, when in the old days a noble woman gave birth to twins of the opposite sex, this was considered to be a propitious thing.
16. Schulte Nordholt 1996: 209.
17. The parade of *ogoh-ogoh* is a relatively recent phenomenon, which happened for the first time in Denpasar in the late 1980s. In 2000 it was held for the first time in Blahkiuh.
18. Interviews in Blahkiuh, September 2003; *Jakarta Post,* 20 Apr. 2004. In two other places in south Bali local violence had also occurred that day.
19. In December 1998 people from the relatively poor villages Cempaga and Sidatapa (PDI-P) in northern Bali clashed with inhabitants from Banjar (richer, Golkar) (*Detik.com,* 14 Dec. 1998), while in south Bali the rival villages of Jagapati and Anggantaka took respectively sides with Golkar and PDI-P.
20. A similar conflict occurred in September 2003 in the village of Sibetan; *Bali Post,* 28 July 2003; *Denpost,* 1 Sept. 2003.
21. *Bali Post,* 12 Aug. 2003; 29 Dec. 2003.
22. These were the Majelis Pembina Lembaga Adat Propinsi at the provincial level, and the Badan Pembinaan dan Penyuluh Lembaga Adat at the district level.
23. Interview with Ketut Sumarta, June 2004. At the provincial level the Majelis Utama Desa Pakraman is established, and in most districts there is at least in name a Majelis Madya, consisting of five *adat* leaders and three so-called *tokoh* (public personalities).
24. *Penduduk Indonesia* 2001, Seri L.2.2: 10.9, 11.1.
25. *ICG* 2003: 8; *Bali Post,* 3 Jan. 2003. Construction workers from Lombok earn Rp. 25,000 per day, whereas Balinese are paid Rp. 50,000.
26. *South China Morning Post,* 3 Apr. 2002
27. *ICG* 2003; *Sarad* 34, 2003.
28. *Bali Post,* 11 Feb. 2003.
29. *Taksu,* May 2004.
30. Widnyani and Widia 2002.
31. See Connor and Vickers 2003: 177–9

Chapter 5

1. See for instance *Kompas,* 8 Feb. 2000, 22 Nov. 2004, 13 Jan. 2005.
2. In 2002 Bali received Rp. 1,539 billion DAU from Jakarta; the total income was Rp. 2,362 billion, and Rp. 1,145 billion was spent on salaries.
3. *Bali Post,* 22 June 2004; *Jakarta Post,* 7 July 2005.
4. Picard 2003; *Kompas,* 12 Mar. 2001.

5. *Bali Post,* 13 Aug. 2003, 4 Sept. 2003.
6. See also *ICG* 2003: 10.
7. *Bali Post,* 30 July 2002, 12 Aug. 2002, 22 Aug. 2002, 20 Sept. 2002, 23 Sept. 2002; official documents of the establishment of Forum Peduli Denpasar, 20 Sept. 2002.
8. *Bali Post,* 10 Jan. 2003.
9. *Bali Post,* 28 July 2003; *Denpost,* 26/28 July 2003, 29 Aug. 2003, 5 Sept. 2003, 6 Sept. 2003; *Fajar Bali,* 26 July 2003.
10. *Radar Bali,* 14/15 May 2004.
11. *Radar Bali,* 2 Apr. 2004; *Denpost,* 30 Apr. 2004.
12. Based on *Bali Post,* 12 Nov. 2003; 12 Feb. 2004; 17 Feb. 2004; *Jawa Pos,* 24 Nov. 2003, 18 Feb. 2004; *Sarad* 45, 2004.
13. *Bali Post,* 14 Sept. 2002, *Radar Bali,* 2/3 Sept. 2003. Kari Subali played also an intimidating role during the trial of an Australian paedophile who committed suicide in Karangasem prison after he was convicted in May 2004 (*Nusa,* 12 May 2004).
14. Because councils elected so-called packages of two candidates — district head and the vice-district head — Sandiyasa participated in two different packages: one with a running mate from his own party and the second with a running mate from Golkar. As a result his two packages obtained respectively 13 and 12 votes. Although he himself obtained 25 votes, neither of his packages reached the necessary 16 votes (50 per cent plus 1).
15. *Kompas,* 15 Aug. 2000; *Apakabar,* 28 Aug. 2000.
16. *Denpost,* 21 July 2003, 26 July 2003, 14 Aug. 2003, 8 Sept. 2003, 20 Sept. 2003, 23 Sept. 2003.
17. *Bali Post,* 17 Nov. 2003.
18. *Tempo,* 28 Dec. 2004/3 Jan. 2005. I was told that Gede Winasa maintained good relationships with a group of Japanese investors. Gede Winasa is also known for his megalomania, including a failed project to convert seawater into drinking water, and one to move the airport of Bali from Badung to his district. For a partisan biography of Gede Winasa, see Nanoq da Kansas 2003.
19. See Lay 2002, Chapter 3; Savirani 2004, Chapter 4.
20. Apart from the youth organisation AMPG, Golkar could also rely on other auxiliary forces like the Laskar Cimande in Denpasar, consisting of young men with a *pencak silat* background (*Bali Post,* 22 July 2003).
21. Golkar hijacked the government slogan *"Bali aman, turis datang"* (When Bali is safe, tourists will come), and changed it into *"Golkar menang, turis datang"* (If Golkar wins, tourists will come).
22. These so-called *studi banding* trips are often nothing more than state-sponsored holidays.
23. Based on interviews in Blahkiuh in September 2003 and June 2004.

24. *Sarad* 44, 2003; *Bali Post,* 28 May 2003, 4 Aug. 2003, 27 Aug. 2003, 5 Sept. 2003; *Denpost,* 28 Aug. 2003, 8 Sept. 2003.
25. *Jakarta Post,* 27 Oct. 2003; *Bali Post,* 27 Oct. 2003, 29 Oct. 2003. The violence in Petandakan had also local roots. The family of the two victims belongs to a small group of people who are slightly better off and had changed their loyalty from PDI-P to Golkar. During the campaign of the elections in 1999 the house of the victims had been attacked as well.
26. *Bali Post,* 12 Nov. 2003, 17 Nov. 2003.

Chapter 6

1. Cf. Connor and Vickers 2003.
2. According to Vickers (2002) few people actually supported the Bali Merdeka movement but many favoured a "Bali for the Balinese" policy.
3. Announcement of the symposium on *H.SEASIA,* 6 June 2000. See for a similar neo-colonial idea that culture is an object that can be programmed and manipulated, Panji Tisna (2001: 24–5): "How about pushing for a critical and objective re-examination of Balinese traditions: maintain those that are beneficial and separate from those that are detrimental."
4. Howe 2001: 83.
5. The *Bali Post* is one of the oldest independent newspapers in Indonesia. It started in 1948 as *Suara Indonesia.* In 1965 it changed its name into *Suluh Indonesia,* and in 1966 in *Suluh Marhaen.* In 1972 the newspaper was renamed for the last time as *Bali Post* (Dwikora Putra and Wayan Supartha 2000). These names reflect nicely the changing orientation from nation to region, although ideologically the newspaper has always been close to PNI and PDI(-P).
6. The daily newspaper *NUSA* was financed by the Bakrie Group and started to circulate shortly after the Bali Nirwana Resort case (see Chapter 2).
7. Couteau 2002. Whereas Satria Naradha claims the sole "authorship" of *Ajeg* Bali, others (Agung Alit 2004) argue that the leader of *puri* Satria and mayor of Denpasar, A.A. Puspayoga, played a major role in conceptualising the idea. Helen Creese informs me that the term "*ajeg*" was already used in 1993 in the context of the conservation of Balinese culture (see Nyoman Sukantha *et al.* 1993: 4).
8. Darma Putra 2003. Bali TV required an investment of Rp. 30 billion and Rp. 500 million per month to keep the business going. Because the audience is relatively small, few firms are willing to advertise on Bali TV (*Pantau* 3, 33, Jan. 2003).
9. Picard 1996; Darma Putra 2003.

10. More and more Balinese say *"Om Swastiastu"* instead of "Hello" when answering their hand phone.
11. According to his critics he is too much of a joker, which undermines the sacred authority of the Brahman priesthood.
12. *Sarad* 43, 2003. Research by Emma Baulch on youth culture in Bali shows that an anti-*Ajeg* Bali movement emphasises international connections through reggae and underground music, whereas a form of "black metal" uses trance elements of Balinese cleansing or *"caru"* practices (presentation at the KNAW conference "Indonesia in Transition", Universitas Indonesia, 27 Aug. 2003).
13. Santikarma 2003.
14. See for instance Made Titib (2005) and the interesting SWOT analysis of Balinese culture by the late Made Kembar Kerepun (2005) in which he compared Bali with Hawaii, where the authentic culture has disappeared.
15. *Bali Post*, 12 Sept. 2003.
16. *Bali Post*, 5 Jan. 2005. The heroes included freedom fighters, nationalist and religious leaders, a dancer, a painter, an architect, an environmentalist, and one foreigner, the American Catholic priest Shadeg who was honoured for his study of the Balinese language.
17. During the commemoration of the Puputan Badung on 20 September 2003 a banner had the slogan: *"Dengan semangat puputan kita kokohkan persatuan dan kesatuan demi ajegnya Bali"* (With the spirit of the *puputan* we reinforce the totality and unity for the sake of the strength of Bali).
18. Personal communication Ngurah Suryawan.
19. See Kembar Kerepun 2005. Also I Gede Pitana, former head of the Department of Tourism in Bali and nowadays Secretary General of the Pasek movement, maintains that Bali is threatened by a steady inflow of Muslims (interview September 2005).

Chapter 7

1. It is interesting to see how terms like "synchronisation", "anticipation", "coordination" and "operation", which formed the military grammar of the New Order bureaucracy, are still used.
2. *Radar Bali*, 29 May 2003; *Bali Post*, 24 June 2004. The running mate of Made Beratha was Alit Kelakan, a young PDI-P cadre who had, in contrast to the PDI elite from *puri* Satria, actively supported Megawati when she was expelled from the PDI in 1996.
3. *Bali Post*, 22 July 2003, 24 July 2003; *Denpost*, 23 July 2003. People referred in this respect, to the 1950s when Megawati's father, President Sukarno, overruled the candidate of the provincial council, Nyoman Mantik, and appointed his own favourite, Sutedja, to be governor of Bali.

4. *Kedaulatan Rakyat,* 16 Aug. 2003; *Bali Post,* 25 July 2003.
5. *Bali Post,* 29 July 2003, 3 Aug. 2003.
6. *Bali Post,* 4 July 2003, 6 Aug. 2003. Mobile phones were collected to guarantee that the 38 PDI-P members were isolated from the outside world.
7. *Bali Post,* 7 Aug. 2003, 11 Aug. 2003. Apparently seven PDI-P members had defected. This could be confirmed because PDI-P members were secretly instructed to write the name of Made Beratha in capital letters on the ballot paper in order to trace their votes.
8. *Tempo,* 18 Aug. 2003; *Radar Bali,* 19 Aug. 2003; *Jakarta Post,* 23 Aug. 2003, 29 Aug. 2003.
9. *Bali Post,* 13 Aug. 2003. Party headquarters immediately denied that they had paid these "costs."
10. *Sarad* 41, 2003. Money from the office of the governor was first transferred to PDI-P headquarters in Jakarta and then distributed among PDI-P assembly members.
11. *Jakarta Post,* 29 Sept. 2003.
12. Darma Putra 2003.
13. *Taksu* V, 112, 2004. In March 2004 small incidents occurred in Tabanan, Sukawati and Bangli; *Radar Bali,* 25 Mar. 2004; *Nusa,* 18 Mar. 2004 and 1 Apr. 2004. Laskar Bali became a militia of the Partai Karya Peduli Bangsa led by Tutut Suharto.
14. This was part of the nation wide economy of the elections. Political parties had to establish a particular number of branches throughout the country in order to participate in the national elections. Usually people were paid to represent these parties at the local level.
15. Website KPU; *Bali Post* and *Nusa,* Apr. 2004.
16. *Sarad* 50, 2004. In Badung Golkar came back from 3.3 per cent to 21.9 per cent.
17. *Denpost,* 17 Apr. 2004 and 20 Apr. 2004; *Radar Bali,* 17 Apr. 2004; *Nusa,* 19 and 29 Apr. 2004; *Warta Bali,* 24 Apr. 2004 and 29 Apr. 2004.
18. *Radar Bali,* 25 June 2004; *Nusa,* 24 June 2004; *Bali Post,* 26 June 2004.
19. Geertz 1966: 61.
20. This section is primarily based on newspaper clippings collected by Ngurah Suryawan and in depth research conducted by I Made Arsana Dwiputra. In addition I Wayan Supartha collected data while I conducted a series of interviews.
21. When the yearly budgets have to be approved, the assemblies still have a strong bargaining position and can demand considerable favours. Law 32/2004 also gives the province opportunities to gain more influence over the districts.

22. Mietzner 2005. He also observed that there was a tendency to cross ethnic and regional constituencies. This happened in Denpasar as well where Balinese candidates tried to gain support from migrant communities.
23. See *Sarad* 62, 2005.
24. *Sarad* 62, 2005.
25. *Sarad* 64, 2005.
26. Ida Bagus Rai Mantra supported a local candidate in a national singing contest on television, and, after winning the contest the singer supported Puspayoga-Mantra.
27. I Wayan Geredeg was supported by Kadek O. who controls a lot of gambling activities. Kari Subali was no longer exclusively tied to PDI-P as he mobilised upon request — and payment — supporters for any of the candidates in Karangasem.
28. See Schulte Nordholt 1996.

Chapter 8

1. *Bali Post,* 14 Oct. 2005.
2. *Berita Rakyat,* July 2005.
3. Bali Post, 3–14 Mar. 2006; <www.jiwamerdekablogspot.com>; personal communication Sita van Bemmelen.
4. Interview with Cok Sawitri, September 2006. The ritual was initiated by Ida Wayan Granoka and was the last of a series that started in 2000. See also *Program Mahkota Mahabajrasandhi,* 2006.
5. The *Bali Post* from 25 September 2006 reported on its front page that government funds and locally raised taxes are moved to private bank accounts.
6. I have borrowed this phrase from Bayly 2004: 2; see also Vickers 2002: 94; Schulte Nordholt 2003: 21–2.
7. *Sarad* 43, 2003.
8. Dick 2005; Connor and Vickers 2003: 168.

Glossary

adat	custom, customary rules
agama	religion
ajeg	strong, upright
ajeg Bali	resilient Bali
Angkatan Muda Partai Golkar (AMPG)	Youth Organisation of Golkar
banjar	hamlet
caru	cleansing
Dana Alokasi Umum (DAU)	administrative funds directly paid by Jakarta to districts and administrative towns
dangdut	popular Indonesian pop music
desa adat	customary village
desa dinas	administrative village
desa pakraman	customary village (since 2001)
Dewan Perwakilan Mass (DPM)	Council Representing the Masses; gang of thugs in Karangasem
Dharma Wacana	talk show by Pedanda Made Gunung on Bali TV
Forum Peduli Denpasar (FPD)	Forum Caring for Denpasar; Denpasar based thugs
Galungan	day when gods and ancestors descent
Garuda Wisnu Kencana	giant (but unfinished) statue of Wisnu sitting on a Garuda bird
Golkar	ruling party during Suharto's New Order

Grebeg Aksara Prasada	cleansing ritual *cum* pilgrimage held in Denpasar 20 September 2006
kasepekang	ostracising someone
kasus adat	adat conflict at village level
kebalian	Balineseness
kembar buncing	twins of the opposite sex
Kooperasi Krama Bali	cooperative of native Balinese small entrepreneurs
kotamadya	administrative town
krama	customary practice; village council
kris	dagger
Krismon	monetary crisis of 1997–98
kulkul	wooden alarm clock
laba pura	temple land
Laskar Bali	gang of thugs based in Denpasar
Majapahit	Javanese kingdom (thirteenth–fifteenth century)
maligia jangkep	post cremation ritual
medharma suaka	friendly visit
melasti	cleansing ritual
merakyat	socialising with the people
niskala	invisible forces
Nyepi	Balinese new year
ogoh-ogoh	huge puppets of ogres carried around the night before Balinese new year
ojek	motor taxi
Pancasila	five pillars of national ideology of Indonesia
PDI	Indonesian Democratic Party
PDI-P	Indonesian Democratic Party of Struggle (1998); political party led by Megawati Sukarnoputri
Pajak Hotel Restoran (PHR)	hotel and restaurant tax
Parisada Hindu Dharma (Indonesia)	semi-government organisation in charge of Balinese and later Indonesian Hinduism
Parisada Campuan	conservative, aristocratic Hindu organisation in Bali (2001)
Parisada Besakih	modernist, egalitarian Hindu organisation in Bali (2001)

Pasek	large commoner descent group
Panca Wali Krama	large all Bali cleansing ritual
pecalang	village police
pedanda	Brahman priest
Peguyuban Tiga Warga	association of commoner groups
pencak silat	martial art
Pendapatan Asli Daerah (PAD)	locally raised taxes
Perda	Peraturan Daerah, regional regulation
PNI	Indonesian Nationalist Party
posko	*pos komando*, local branches of political parties
prasasti	stone inscription/declaration signed by authorities
Puputan Badung	heroic suicidal resistance of the kings of Badung against the Dutch in September 1906
pura	temple
puri	noble house
Raad Kerta	customary court in colonial period
Reformasi	period of political reform following Suharto's demise (1998–2001)
ruko	a combination of a shop and a house
Rupiah	Indonesian currency
sawah	rice field
sekala	the visible world
sinetron	soap series on TV
subak	irrigation association
Tri Hita Karana	balance between gods, men and environment
warga	commoner's descent group
warung	coffee shop/foodstall

Bibliography

Aditjondro, George Junus. 1995. *Bali: Jakarta's Colony. Social and Ecological Impacts of Jakarta-based Conglomerates in Bali's Tourist Industry.* Perth: Asia Research Centre, Murdoch University. [Working paper 58]

Agung Alit. 2004. "Praying Contests". *Latitudes* 42.

Ardana, I Ketut. 2004. "Puri dan Politik: Reformasi Nasional dan Dinamika Politik Regional Bali". In I Nyoman Darma Putra (ed.), *Bali Menuju Jagaditha: Aneka Perspektif,* pp. 34–52. Denpasar: Pustaka Bali Post.

Aspinall, Eward and Greg Fealy (eds.). 2003. *Local Power and Politics in Indonesia: Decentralisation and Democratisation.* Singapore: Institute of Southeast Asian Studies.

Bakker, Frederik Lambertus. 1993. *The Struggle of the Hindu Balinese Intellectuals: Developments in Modern Hindu Thinking in Independent Indonesia.* Amsterdam: VU University Press.

Bali Beyond the Tragedy. 2003. *Impact and Challenges for Tourism Led Development in Indonesia.* Jakarta: UNPDP/USAID/World Bank.

Bali Membangun 2002. 2003. Denpasar: Bappeda.

Bateson, Gregory. 1970. "Bali: The Value System of a Steady State". In Jane Belo (ed.), *Traditional Balinese Culture,* pp. 384–401. New York: Columbia University Press.

Bayly, Christopher. 2004. *The Birth of the Modern World 1780–1914.* Oxford: Blackwell.

Couteau, Jean. 2002. "Bali: Crise en paradis", *Archipel* 64: 231–54.

Connor, Linda and Adrian Vickers. 2003. "Crisis, Citizenship, and Cosmopolitanism: Living in a Local and Global Risk Society in Bali". *Indonesia* 75: 153–80.

Darma Putra, I Nyoman. 2003. "Bali Pasca-bom: Konflik, Kekerasan dan Rekonstruksi Identitas Budaya Menuju 'Ajeg Bali'." Paper presented at the Kongres Kebudayaan in Bukittinggi, 19–23 October.

Dick, Howard. 2005. "Southeast Asia as an Open System: Geopolitics and Economic Geography". In Paul Kratoska, Remco Raben, and Henk Schulte Nordholt (eds.), *Locating Southeast Asia: Geographies of Knowledge and the Politics of Space*, pp. 250–74. Singapore: Singapore University Press/Leiden: KITLV Press.

Dwikora, Putra and Wayan Supartha (eds.). 2000. *K. Nadha: Sang Perintis*. Denpasar: Pustaka Bali Post.

Erb, M, Priambudi Sulistiyanto and C. Faucher (eds.). 2005. *Regionalism in Post Suharto Indonesia*. London: RoutledgeCurzon.

Geertz, Clifford. 1966. *Person, Time, and Conduct in Bali: An Essay in Cultural Analysis*. New Haven: Yale University Southeast Asia Studies. Cultural Report Series 14.

Howe, Leo. 2001. *Hinduism and Hierarchy in Bali*. Oxford: James Curry/ Santa Fe: School of American Research Press.

International Crisis Group (ICG). 2003. *The Perils of Private Security in Indonesia: Guards and Militias on Bali and Lombok*. Jakarta/Brussels: International Crisis Group.

Kembar Kerepun, Made. 2005. "Analisis S.W.O.T. Dalam Strategi Mencapai dan Memelihara Ajeg Bali". In I Made Titib (ed.), *Dialog Ajeg Bali: Perspectif Pengalaman Agama Hindu*, pp. 41–104. Surabaya: Paramita.

Lay, C. 2002. *Eksekutif dan Legislatif di Daerah: Penelitian Tentang Potensi Konflik Antara DPRD dan Birokrasi di Daerah*. Jakarta: Kementerian Riset dan Teknologi/LIPI.

MacRae, Graeme S. 1997. "Economy, Ritual and History in a Balinese Tourist Town" (PhD thesis, University of Auckland).

Magenda, Burhan. 1989. "The Surviving Aristocracy in Indonesia: Politics in Three Provinces of the Outer Islands" (PhD thesis, Cornell University), 2 vols.

Malley, Michael. 1999. "Regions; Centralisation and Resistance". In Donald Emmerson (ed.), *Indonesia Beyond Suharto*, pp. 71–105. New York: Armonk/London: Sharpe.

Mietzner, Marcus. 2005. "Local Democracy", *Inside Indonesia* 65: 17–18.

Nanoq da Kansas. 2003. *Anak Desa Penantang Zaman: Biografi Singkat Prof. Dr. Drg. I Gede Winasa*. Negara: Komunitas Kertas Budaya.

Ngurah Bagus, I G. 2004. "The Parisada Hindu Dharma Indonesia in a Society in Transformation: The Emergence of Conflicts Amidst Differences and Demands". In Martin Ramstedt (ed.), *Hinduism in Modern Indonesia: A Minority Religion Between Local, National, and Global Interests*, pp. 84–92. London/New York: RoutledgeCurzon.

Panji Tisna, I G. Raka. 2001. "The Loss of the Last Paradise: Nature — Culture and the Economic Temptation". In Urs Ramseyer and I G. Raka Panji Tisna (eds.), *Bali. Living in Two Worlds: A Critical*

Self-portrait, pp. 15–26. Basel: Verlag Schwabe & Co./Museum der Kulturen.

Parimartha, I Gde. 2003. *Memahami Desa Adat, Desa Dinas dan Desa Pakraman: Suatu Tinjauan Historis, Kritis.* Denpasar: Universitas Udayana. [Inaugural Lecture]

Pemberton, John. 1994. *On the Subject of* "Java". Ithaca/London: Cornell University Press.

Penduduk Indonesia. 2001. *Hasil Sensus Penduduk Tahun 2000.* Jakarta: BPS. [Seri L.2.2]

Picard, Michel. 1996. *Bali: Cultural Tourism and Touristic Culture.* Singapore: Archipelago Press.

———. 1999. "The Discourse of Kebalian: Transcultural Constructions of Balinese Identity". In Raechelle Rubinstein and Linda H. Connors (eds.), *Staying Local in the Global Village: Bali in the Twentieth Century*, pp. 15–49. Honolulu: University of Hawai'i Press.

———. 2003. "Touristification and Balinisation in a Time of Reformasi". *Indonesia and the Malay World* 31: 108–18.

———. 2005. "Otonomi Daerah in Bali: The Call for Special Autonomy Status in the Name of Kebalian". In Maribeth Erb, Priyambudi Sulistiyanto and Carole Faucher (eds.), *Regionalism in Post-Suharto Indonesia*, pp. 111–24. London: RoutledgeCurzon.

Pigeaud, Theodore G. Th. 1938. *Javaansch-Nederlandsch Handwoordenboek.* Groningen/Batavia: J.B.Wolters.

Pitana, I Gde. 1999. "Status Struggles and the Priesthood in Contemporary Bali." In Raechelle Rubinstein and Linda H. Connors (eds.), *Staying Local in the Global Village: Bali in the Twentieth Century*, pp. 181–201. Honolulu: University of Hawai'i Press.

———. 2001. "Sociology of the Temple: Issues Related to Rivalry in Status and Power". In Urs Ramseyer and I G. Raka Panji Tisna (eds.), *Bali. Living in Two Worlds: A Critical Self-portrait*, pp. 117–27. Basel: Verlag Schwabe & Co./Museum der Kulturen.

Pringle, Robert. 2004. *A Short History of Bali.* Crows Nest: Allen and Unwin.

———. 2006. *Program Mahkota Mahabajrasandhi. Menuju Puncak Kemegahan.* N.p., n. publ..

Ramstedt, Martin. 2002. "Hinduism in modern Indonesia". In Satish Chandra and Baladas Ghoshal (eds.), *Indonesia: A New Beginning?*, pp. 140–68. New Delhi: Sterling Publishers.

———. 2004. "Negotiating Identities: Indonesian 'Hindus' Between Local, National, and Global Interests". In Martin Ramstedt (ed.), *Hinduism in Modern Indonesia: A Minority Religion Between Local, National, and Global Interests*, pp. 1–34. London/New York: RoutledgeCurzon.

Rhoades, Elizabeth. 2007. "Bali standing strong." *Inside Indonesia* 89.

Robinson, Geoffrey. 1995. *The Dark Side of Paradise: Political Violence in Bali*. Ithaca/London: Cornell University Press.

Santikarma, Degung. 2001a. "The Power of Balinese culture". In Urs Ramseyer and I G. Raka Panji Tisna (eds.), *Bali. Living in Two Worlds: A Critical Self-portrait*, pp. 27–45. Basel: Verlag Schwabe & Co./Museum der Kulturen.

————. 2001b. "The Burden of Being Exotic". *Latitudes* 1.

————. 2002. "Pecalang: Siaga Budaya atau Membudayakan Siaga?" *Kompas* 29 Sept. 2002.

————. 2003. "Ajeg Bali: Dari Gadis Cilik ke Made Schwarzenegger". *Kompas* 7 Dec. 2003.

Satria Naradha (ed.). 2004. *Ajeg Bali: Sebuah Cita-cita*. Denpasar: Bali Post.

Savirani, L. 2004. "Local Strongmen in New Regional Politics in Indonesia" (MA thesis, International School for Social Sciences and the Humanities, University of Amsterdam).

Schulte Nordholt, Henk. 1996. *The Spell of Power: A History of Balinese Politics 1650–1940*. Leiden: KITLV Press.

————. 1999. "The Making of Traditional Bali: Colonial Ethnography and Bureaucratic Reproduction". In Peter Pels and Oscar Salemink (eds.), *Colonial Subjects: Essays on the Practical History of Anthropology*, pp. 241–81. Ann Arbor: University of Michigan Press.

————. 2001. "Plotting Time in Bali: Articulating Plurality". In Willem van Schendel and Henk Schulte Nordholt (eds.), *Time Matters: Global and Local Time in Asian Societies*, pp. 57–76. Amsterdam: VU University Press.

————. 2003. "Introduction". In Henk Schulte Nordholt and Gusti Asnan (eds.), *Indonesia in Transition: Work in Progress*, pp. 1–24. Jogjakarta: Pustaka Pelajar.

Schulte Nordholt, Henk and Gerry van Klinken (eds.). 2007. *Renegotiating Boundaries: Local Politics in Post Suharto Indonesia*. Leiden: KITLV Press.

Smith-Kipp, Rita. 1993. *Dissociated Identities; Ethnicity, Religion, and Class in an Indonesian Society*. Ann Arbor: University of Michigan Press.

Statistik Keuangan. 2003. *Statistik Keuangan Pemerintah Daerah, Kabupaten dan Kota 2000–2002*. Denpasar: Pemda Bali.

Suasta, Putu. 2001. "Between Holy Waters and Highways". In Urs Ramseyer and I G. Raka Panji Tisna (eds.), *Bali. Living in Two Worlds: A Critical Self-portrait*, pp. 37–44. Basel: Verlag Schwabe & Co./Museum der Kulturen.

Suasta, Putu and Linda Connor. 1999. "Democratic Mobilisation and Political Authoritarianism: Tourism Developments on Bali". In Raechelle Rubinstein and Linda H. Connor (eds.), *Staying Local in the Global Village: Bali in the Twentieth Century*, pp. 91–122. Honolulu: University of Hawai'i Press.

Subandi, Ketut. 1982. *Sapta Rsi Dengan Perkembangan Dari Masa ka Masa.* Denpasar: Maha Gotra Pasek Sanak Sapta Rsi.

Sukartha, Nyoman, Ida Bagus Mayun and I Wayan Rupa. 1993. *Peranan Mabebasan Dalam Menyebarluaskan Nilai-nilai Budaya Masyarakat Bali.* Jakarta: Departemen Pendidikan dan Kebudayaan.

Titib, I Made (ed.). 2005. *Dialog Ajeg Bali: Perspectif Pengalaman Agama Hindu.* Surabaya: Paramita.

Vickers, Adrian. 2002. "Bali Merdeka? Internal Migration, Tourism and Hindu Revivalism". In Minako Sakai (ed.), *Beyond Jakarta: Regional Autonomy and Local Society in Indonesia*, pp. 80–100. Adelaide: Crawford House.

Warren, Carol. 1994. *Centre and Periphery in Indonesia: Environment, Politics and Human Rights in the Regional Press (Bali).* Perth: Asia Research Centre, Murdoch University. [Working paper no. 42]

———. 2000. "Adat and the Discourse of Modernity in Bali". In A.Vickers and I Nyoman Darma Putra (eds.), *To Change Bali: Essays in Honour of I G Ngurah Bagus*, pp. 1–14. Denpasar: Bali Post.

———. 2004. "Adat-Balinese Discourse and Practice: Locating Citizenship and the Commonweal". [Unpublished paper]

Widnyani, Nyoman and I Ketut Widia. 2002. *Pecalang Desa Pakraman Bali.* Denpasar: SIC.

Newpapers/Newsgroups

Apakabar/Clarknet
Asia Times
Bali Arts and Culture Newsletter (BACN)
Bali Post
Berita Rakyat (Banyuwangi)
Bogbog
Denpost
Detik.com
Fajar Bali
Far Eastern Economic Review (FEER)
Jakarta Post
Jawa Pos
Jiwamerdekablogspot.com

Kedaulatan Rakyat (Jogjakarta)
Kompas
Newsweek
Nusa
Pantau
Radar Bali
Sarad
South China Morning Post
Suara Merdeka
Taksu
Tempo
Warta Bali

Index